ARTHUR MILLER'S

The Crucible

BY

William Bly
Assistant Professor of Drama
New York University

SERIES EDITOR

Michael Spring
Editor, *Literary Cavalcade*
Scholastic Inc.

BARRON'S EDUCATIONAL SERIES, INC.
Woodbury, New York / London / Toronto / Sydney

ACKNOWLEDGMENTS
We would like to acknowledge the many painstaking hours of work Holly Hughes and Thomas F. Hirsch have devoted to making the *Book Notes* series a success.

© Copyright 1984 by Barron's Educational Series, Inc.

All inquiries should be addressed to:
Barron's Educational Series, Inc.
113 Crossways Park Drive
Woodbury, New York 11797

Library of Congress Catalog Card No. 84-18438

International Standard Book No. 0-8120-3408-2

Library of Congress Cataloging in Publication Data
Bly, William.
　Arthur Miller's The Crucible.

　(Barron's book notes)
　Bibliography: p. 103
　Summary: A guide to reading "The Crucible" with a critical and appreciative mind. Includes background on the author's life and times, sample tests, term paper suggestions, and a reading list.

　1. Miller, Arthur, 1915–　. The Crucible. [1. Miller, Arthur, 1915–　. The crucible. 2. American literature —History and criticism] I. Title.
PS3525.I5156C733　1984　　812'.8　　84-18438
ISBN 0-8120-3408-2 (pbk.)

PRINTED IN THE UNITED STATES OF AMERICA

456　　550　　98765432

881452

CONTENTS

HOW TO USE THIS BOOK

You have to know how to approach literature in order to get the most out of it. This *Barron's Book Notes* volume follows a plan based on methods used by some of the best students to read a work of literature.

Begin with the guide's section on the author's life and times. As you read, try to form a clear picture of the author's personality, circumstances, and motives for writing the work. This background usually will make it easier for you to hear the author's tone of voice, and follow where the author is heading.

Then go over the rest of the introductory material—such sections as those on the plot, characters, setting, themes, and style of the work. Underline, or write down in your notebook, particular things to watch for, such as contrasts between characters and repeated literary devices. At this point, you may want to develop a system of symbols to use in marking your text as you read. (Of course, you should only mark up a book you own, not one that belongs to another person or a school.) Perhaps you will want to use a different letter for each character's name, a different number for each major theme of the book, a different color for each important symbol or literary device. Be prepared to mark up the pages of your book as you read. Put your marks in the margins so you can find them again easily.

Now comes the moment you've been waiting for—the time to start reading the work of literature. You may want to put aside your *Barron's Book Notes* volume until you've read the work all the way through. Or you may want to alternate, reading the *Book Notes* analysis of each section as soon as you have finished reading the corresponding part of the original. Before you move on, reread crucial passages you don't fully understand. (Don't take this guide's analysis for granted—make up your own mind as to what the work means.)

Once you've finished the whole work of literature, you may want to review it right away, so you can firm up your ideas about what it means. You may want to leaf through the book concentrating on passages you marked in reference to one character or one theme. This is also a good time to reread the *Book Notes* introductory material, which pulls together insights on specific topics.

When it comes time to prepare for a test or to write a paper, you'll already have formed ideas about the work. You'll be able to go back through it, refreshing your memory as to the author's exact words and perspective, so that you can support your opinions with evidence drawn straight from the work. Patterns will emerge, and ideas will fall into place; your essay question or term paper will almost write itself. Give yourself a dry run with one of the sample tests in the guide. These tests present both multiple-choice and essay questions. An accompanying section gives answers to the multiple-choice questions as well as suggestions for writing the essays. If you have to select a term paper topic, you may choose one from the list of suggestions in this book. This guide also provides you with a reading list, to help you when you start research for a term paper, and a selection of provocative comments by critics, to spark your thinking before you write.

THE AUTHOR AND HIS TIMES

In Salem, Massachusetts, a dozen teen-age girls and a black slave woman are caught dancing in the woods around a bubbling cauldron. Today, you wouldn't even use the word "caught." You might think these girls were strange, but you'd hardly call the cops on them. But it's 1692, and Salem isn't just an ordinary small town; it's a religious community of the strictest kind. The people and their laws are as harsh as the Massachusetts winter. When two of the girls pass out from fright and can't be revived, the others find themselves in serious trouble. Women who dance with the Devil are witches; and witches, when they are caught, are hanged. To get themselves out of their predicament, the girls try to spread the blame around. But the blame-spreading gets out of hand, and before long the whole town is in a panic, everyone accusing everyone else of witchcraft. Nineteen people will be hanged before the madness is stopped.

Well, you say, people were superstitious then. Nothing like that could happen today. Maybe so, but in the early 1950s, at the time *The Crucible* was written, a similar kind of hunt was taking place, not for witches, but for Communists. Today it bears the harmless-sounding name of the McCarthy Hearings on Un-American Activities, but for the people who got caught up in it—some of them our parents and grandparents—this "witch-hunt" was anything but harmless. In fact, to the playwright Arthur Miller, the

McCarthy Hearings bore an alarming resemblance to the trials in Salem in 1692. *The Crucible* was his way of trying to keep history from repeating itself.

One of the most popular TV shows in 1953 was "I Led Three Lives." It always began the same way: A man's face appears on the screen. His expression is taut with anxiety. The narrator says something like, "This is the fantastically true story of Herbert A. Philbrick, who for nine frightening years did lead three lives—average citizen, member of the Communist Party, and counterspy for the FBI. For obvious reasons, the names, dates and places have been changed, but the story is based on fact." The show was scary and exciting, but it always left you worried, because Philbrick's job never seemed to be done. Communist spies were everywhere, and one man could do only so much against so many.

There was a lot of talk in those days about the "Red Menace." Red is the color of the Russian flag, and all Russians are Communists. So to say "Better dead than red" meant that you'd kill yourself before you let the Communists take over. The slogan was repeated over and over throughout America. My father said it; my teachers said it; I'm sure I said it myself, even though I was just five years old at the time.

And in fact there were good reasons to be worried about the Russians. They had the atomic bomb, as we did. But a lot of people said they got the bomb by using spies, and that really made us worry. It was charged that secret agents, working under cover, had stolen our secrets and given them to the Enemy. Even worse, these spies supposedly were hardly ever Russians themselves, but often American citizens, as normal as you or me, the kind of people you see every day on the street and hardly even notice. Blacks are identifiable by their skin color; foreigners speak with an unusual accent. But a Communist could be anybody. It sort of makes a Communist sound like the bogey-man, doesn't it? Well, to many people in 1953, a Communist was just as scary as the bogey-man, and a lot more real.

Soon after it was discovered that the Russians had the bomb, the U.S. Congress started investigations into so-called Un-American Activities, and one of the men they put in charge was Joseph R. McCarthy, a senator from Wisconsin. McCarthy claimed America was in great danger from a Communist conspiracy to take over the world. And, as if he were a surgeon hacking away tumors in a body riddled with cancer, he tried to root out every trace of Communism he could find. It soon became clear that very few people were *completely* free of any connection with Communism. To find out why, we have to go back in time a little bit.

Arthur Miller had just turned 14 when his family's savings were wiped out by the stock market crash of October, 1929. Almost literally overnight, the lives of many of his friends changed from reasonable comfort to poverty. Over the next 12 years—the time of the Great Depression, as it is called—Arthur Miller came to know and work with people who had joined the Communist Party. These people weren't spies, they simply were desperate, and they saw Communism as a way out of a desperate situation. And although Communism worried a few people in the 1930s, most were too busy with their own problems to give it much thought. Besides, Soviet Russia was not yet an enemy of the United States. In fact, Russian and American soldiers later fought side by side against the Germans at the end of World War II. It wasn't until after the war, when—as so often happens—the victors turned against each other, that Communism began to be considered a very serious threat.

By the late 1940s when the Congressional hearings first began, there were quite a few people who had flirted with Communism at some time or other, although most had renounced it long before. But even if you had no Communism in your own past, you could easily be in the same position as Arthur Miller—you knew someone who did. That was more than enough to get you in trouble with Senator McCarthy and similar investigators.

Imagine what it was like being called in to testify. McCarthy or his aides might say, "Are you now, or have you ever been, a member of the Communist Party?" No. "Do you know anyone who is or was a Communist?" No. McCarthy holds up some cards. "We have the names of people who have already confessed. Your name came up in connection with their testimony. Why do you suppose that is?" You say you don't know, but you can tell that no one believes you. Maybe you're not so innocent after all, you think. Maybe you've been sucked into the conspiracy without realizing it. Have you signed anything, donated any money, said anything to anybody that might sound suspicious?

Once you start thinking like this, it's almost impossible to stop. You begin to feel guilty either way: even if you don't have any Communist connections, you've done nothing to stop the spread of this evil; you may have even helped the enemy by being stupid or naïve. *You* did it, it's *your* fault, their questions seem to say. And they won't let you go until you make up for it in some way. So you tell them about your friend who's never home on Tuesday nights, or your mother's uncle who used to quote Communist slogans all the time, or anyone you know who's been acting a little odd the last few weeks. You name names, and they let you go.

And afterward no one wants anything to do with you. You were called in to testify, there had to be a reason. You must be a Communist, or at least have been working for them. You lose your friends, your job, sometimes even your family. You become an outcast. Your life is ruined.

This was the fate of many innocent people. Those who were spared either joined in the witch-hunt or kept silent for fear the same thing would happen to them. A lot of the victims never recovered, even long after the rest of the country lost interest and Joe McCarthy had been discredited. By 1957 it was pretty much over, and America could look back with a sad smile, wondering how anyone could have been so foolish.

But in 1953 it was no joke. Arthur Miller already knew about the Salem witch trials from his college days at the University of Michigan (1934–38). In *The Theater Essays of Arthur Miller* he describes how *The Crucible* took shape in his mind: ". . . when the McCarthy era came along," he says, "I remembered these stories and I used to tell them to people when it [the investigation] started. I used to say, you know, McCarthy is actually saying certain lines that I recall the witch-hunters saying in Salem. So I started to go back, not with the idea of writing a play, but to refresh my own mind because it was getting eerie" (p. 290).

One day, while he was reading some documents in the Salem museum, some tourists came in and wanted to see the pins. There was no need to ask, "What pins?" During the trials in 1692, the so-called witches often "sent out their spirits" to stick pins into the flesh of the girls who were accusing them. Now, as Arthur Miller watched, "the tourists pass the books, the exhibits, and no hint of danger reaches them from the quaint relics. I have a desire to tell them the significance of those relics. It is the desire to write" (p. 28).

The significance of those relics was, in part, that the same thing that happened in 1692 was happening all over again. "It was not only the rise of 'McCarthyism' that moved me," he writes, "but something which seemed much more weird and mysterious. It was the fact that a political, objective, knowledgeable campaign from the far Right [Communists were said to be on the far left] was capable of creating not only a terror, but a new subjective reality . . . and that such manifestly ridiculous men [as Senator Joe McCarthy] should be capable of paralyzing thought itself. . . . It was as though the whole country had been born anew, without a memory. . . . Astounded, I watched men pass me by without a nod whom I had known rather well for years. . . ." And so Arthur Miller began to write *The Crucible*.

A few years before, Arthur Miller had become famous. His second play, *Death of a Salesman*, had won the 1949 Pulitzer Prize and a host of other awards. By the time he was 37, in 1952, he was a respected writer of established reputation, and people were looking forward to his next play. What he had to say was bound to be important.

There's a saying that a prophet is honored everywhere except in his own country. This could certainly be said of the author of *The Crucible* when it first opened on Broadway on January 22, 1953. No one missed the parallels between 1692 Salem and 1953 America. "But," many said, "witches never did exist, then or now. Communists are real." Some critics complained that the play was too cold and intellectual. Others said it wasn't a play at all, but some kind of outburst, a political speech. Most people found a way of saying that it wasn't worth bothering with. The play ran for a few months, playing to almost empty houses. Then it closed. But the witch-hunt went on.

Arthur Miller had drawn a lot of attention to himself, and he soon got into trouble. In 1954 he was denied a passport to see a production of *The Crucible* in Belgium. In 1955 the New York City Youth Board began an investigation into his political beliefs. In 1956 he was called on to testify before the House Committee on Un-American Activities. He refused to name names. He was cited for contempt of Congress. He was finally exonerated by the courts, but not until 1958. By then, more and more people were refusing to testify against others, and the witch-hunt was running out of steam. The hearings had gone on for ten years, and the country's attention span was near its end. In all that time, no real Communist conspiracy was ever uncovered. Just as no real witches were ever found in Salem.

Another important thing happened in 1958: *The Crucible* was put on again, this time in a small Off-Broadway theater. "The same critics reviewed it again," Arthur Miller remembers, and "this time they were fairly swept away, the drama was as real to them [now, in 1958] as it had been cold and undramatic before [in 1953]. Reasons were given for the new impression; the main one was that the script had been improved." Miller hadn't changed a word in the script. He began to think that the real reason had more to do with the audience than the play: ". . .

when McCarthyism was around, the . . . audience [was] quite simply in fear of the theme of the play, which was witch-hunting. In [1958] they were not afraid of it, and they began to look at the play" (*Theater Essays*, p. 245).

Most of the time when an author writes a play about current events, the play is forgotten as soon as the events are over. But *The Crucible* has come to be produced more often than even *Death of a Salesman*, which was long considered to be Arthur Miller's most important play. Let's see if we can figure out why.

If you're watching a really scary film, say, *The Exorcist*, you can always reassure yourself by saying, "It's only a movie." But you can't do that with *The Crucible*. The witch-hunt really happened. You can go to Salem today and still find the house where Rebeccah Nurse lived, and see the door through which she was carried to her trial because she was too old and sick to walk. You can stand on the rock where the gallows was built, and look out over Salem Bay, the same bay 19 "witches" must have looked at just before they were hanged. You can go to the courthouse and they'll show you the pins.

Nowadays we don't believe in witches or the Devil, at least we say we don't. But we're still fascinated by the idea of supernatural forces and beings. And, for most of us, the scarier the better. The popularity of horror movies comes from this fascination. *The Crucible* also tells a strange and scary story. But in this play it's not witches or demons that scare us—it's people. Arthur Miller's characters are ordinary folk. The terror that sweeps over them like a wave is real; the people who were hanged really died. In *The Crucible* there are no real witches; so what, then, "possessed" these people?

If you've ever built a wood fire, you know it doesn't start itself. And the biggest logs won't burn right away; you have to begin with smaller sticks, the kindling. But there can be no fire at all without a spark to set the kindling burning.

We can think of the Salem witchcraft as a kind of fire which, once started, could not be quenched until it had burned itself out.

By this analogy, the big logs would be the belief in witchcraft itself. This belief was an old one. In the ancient world, sorcery was everywhere—in Egypt and Babylon, even among the clear-thinking Greeks and the otherwise sensible Romans. Only the Jews, among all these ancient peoples, had laws forbidding the practice of witchcraft. It is first mentioned in the Old Testament (Exodus 22:18), where it says, "Thou shalt not suffer a witch to live." It was on the authority of this one sentence in the Bible that the 19 witches were hanged in Salem in 1692.

But until the end of the Middle Ages, no one had made a "scientific" study of the spirit world, and ideas about witches varied wildly from place to place and century to century. Then in 1486 two Christian monks brought out a book called the *Malleus Maleficarum* (*The Hammer of Witches*), the first book of demonology. Others soon followed (King James I of England even wrote one himself), and by the time Reverend Hale walked into Salem in 1692 with an armload of such books, the study of witchcraft was considered an exact science. When he says of his books, "Here is all the invisible world, caught, defined, and calculated," he is being sincere. He has studied these books for years and he honestly believes himself to be an expert. So does everyone else. There is no reason to doubt him or his ability to deal with an enemy he knows so much about. Without this solid and specific belief in the reality of witchcraft, there might have been only a little brushfire in Salem.

The kindling of the fire was to be found in the visible world. In 1623 King James I (the same one who wrote the demonology book) had granted a charter to the Massachusetts Bay Colony, under which the Puritans could own their own land. This charter enabled the colony to thrive and grow over the next 60 years. But in 1684 the King revoked this charter, saying the land belonged to the Crown, thereby making the Puritans' land titles null and void. A lot of squabbling resulted, finally coming to a head in 1689 when the Puritans overthrew the royal governor and reinstated the old charter. But they knew they had no legal right to do this, and by 1692 the insecurity of their position had taken its toll on their nerves.

Ownership of land wasn't the only issue. The Puritans had come to Massachusetts in the first place not only to avoid religious persecution in England, as the history books say, but to establish a New Jerusalem, God's "visible Kingdome" on Earth. For this reason it was natural for the Puritans to assume that God's archenemy Satan would single them out for his most ferocious attacks. In fact, when witchcraft first broke out, many believed it to be the beginning of Armageddon, the great battle between Darkness and Light that would signal the end of the world. But even before this, the Puritans had already spent several years in constant and growing anxiety about the future of God's "visible Kingdome."

There remains but the spark to set these dry sticks ablaze. The Puritans could hardly have picked a more difficult place to found their New Jerusalem. The ground was full of rocks, the winters were long and bitterly cold, and the forests surrounding their towns were infested with Indians, who continually raided the outlying farms. But the Puritans prospered by banding together. This process not only helped them overcome danger and difficulty but it gave them ample opportunity for minding each other's business.

To the Puritans, man was a creature steeped in sin, and there was nothing he could do to save himself from the eternal fires of hell. A few believers—the elect, as the Puritans called themselves—God had chosen to save, or "justify." Because God had justified them already, the elect naturally obeyed his laws. But you could outwardly obey these laws yet still not be saved. Puritan preachers never tired of railing against the "meritmongers," those who thought they could buy their way into heaven with good works. On the other hand, it was easy to prove that you were damned—all you had to do was break the law. So there was tremendous pressure on everyone at least to *appear* to be one of the elect.

All of this is complicated, even to an adult. But put yourself in the place of a nine-year-old girl named Betty Parris. All you know is that the winter has been long and boring, that the grownups are more cranky than usual so they punish you more often, and that you must have sinned with your teeth because one of them aches. If all this isn't enough, you have to be better than the other children in Salem Village, because your father is the minister. For weeks now your older cousin Abigail Williams has been making you sit with her and listen to your father's slave Tituba tell shocking stories of her former life as a heathen in the Barbados. It was bad enough with just the two of you, but Abby never could keep a secret, and now there are ten or twelve of her friends who turn up at the back door as soon as your father walks out the front, begging Tituba for more. At first it was exciting, in a scary sort of way, but lately Tituba's taken to acting out her heathen rituals, showing how they used to conjure spirits to foretell the future. You know you're damned if you keep this up, but Abby's slammed the door on your only way out: she'll kill you if you tell. Your soul is suffocating in sin, and you can't sleep any more for fear of the nightmares that always come.

The pressure was enough to give anyone a nervous breakdown. Betty Parris "freaked out." Abigail Williams, for all her daring, wasn't immune, and soon she began trying to fly and bursting into howls whenever her uncle prayed aloud or read the Scriptures, just like her cousin Betty. Then Betty, in one of her fits, let slip the name Tituba, and . . . but this is where the play starts.

The Play

The Plot

It's the spring of 1692. The whole village of Salem is in an uproar. The Reverend Samuel Parris' daughter Betty won't wake up, and the Putnams' little Ruth is walking around like a zombie. The night before, Reverend Parris had heard a funny noise in the woods outside his house, and stumbled onto a frightening scene: his black slave Tituba was waving her arms over a boiling kettle, muttering wild-sounding gibberish, and around the fire a dozen girls were dancing— *dancing*, strictly forbidden by Puritan law. Among the girls were Betty and Ruth and his niece Abigail Williams. When he jumped out on them, everyone screamed and ran, all except Betty, who fainted dead away. And now she won't wake up.

The house is buzzing with people, and every other word is "witchcraft." Reverend Parris doesn't want to believe it, but he's sent for an expert just in case—the Reverend John Hale of the neighboring village of Beverly. When Hale arrives he tries to wake Betty, but she remains lifeless. Then he questions Abigail and Tituba. Some of the other village folk who look on are skeptical about witchcraft, especially John Proctor, whose serving girl, Mary Warren, had been with the girls the night before. Whip the nonsense out of them, Proctor suggests. Another doubter is old Rebecca Nurse, "twenty-six times a grandma," who believes the girls are just going through one of their "silly seasons."

But Reverend Hale's questions are so sharp, and Tituba is so scared for her beloved Betty, that she blurts out that she was conjuring the dead. And when Hale presses her, she realizes her only way out is to "confess." She gets carried away and begins to name others that she "saw with the Devil." Soon Abigail is swept up in Tituba's ecstatic "confession," and she too names names. Betty wakes up and joins them.

In the next few days other girls—including Mary Warren—are added to their number, and within a week they have "cried out" (as they called it) 14 "witches." An official court has been set up. John Proctor is particularly worried about Abigail Williams, who has become the girls' ringleader. Abigail had been his maidservant before Mary Warren. When John's wife, Elizabeth, fell ill, he had turned to Abigail in his loneliness, and at least once made love with her in the barn. He repented it immediately, and confessed to Elizabeth, who put Abigail out of the house. Now Proctor is afraid that Abigail means to "dance with him on his wife's grave." He doesn't believe in witches, and he knows what mischief Abigail is capable of, so he decides to go to the court and denounce her. But before he can leave, the marshalls come to arrest Elizabeth: Abigail has "cried her out."

By now the jail is bursting with "witches," and no one seems safe. Rebecca Nurse, the most respectable person in the village, has been convicted and sentenced to hang. John Proctor brings Mary Warren to the court with a statement saying it's all pretense. This is a serious accusation, and the judges—Hathorne and Deputy Governor Danforth—want proof. So Proctor confesses his lechery with Abigail; but when Elizabeth is brought in to corroborate the charge, she denies it, thinking to spare her husband's name. Then

Abigail and the other girls turn on Mary Warren and cry her out. Her resolve collapses and she renounces her statement. Proctor "witched her" into writing it, she says. Proctor is hauled off to jail.

By October, 11 witches have gone to the gallows. On the morning John Proctor and seven others—including Rebecca Nurse—are to hang, strange rumors are going around. Other towns have risen up against their witch courts and overthrown them. Reverend Hale, who had believed John Proctor's story and had denounced the proceedings when Proctor was arrested, has now returned, and he's trying to get the prisoners to "confess" and save their lives, even if it means lying. Perhaps worst of all, Abigail Williams has disappeared, but not before breaking into her uncle's strongbox and stealing all his money. Despite rising doubt in the town, Danforth and Hathorne refuse to call off the executions, because such an action will imply that they murdered the 11 that have already hanged. Their only hope is to get John Proctor to confess. So they bring in his wife, Elizabeth, now four months pregnant, to persuade him. At first Proctor gives in, but when he realizes they want to use his name to save their own skins, he rips up his confession and goes to his death with a clear conscience.

The Characters

John Proctor

If you were to ask one of John Proctor's sons what he wants to be when he grows up, he'd probably say, "My daddy." It's hard to imagine a better role model for a little boy than John Proctor. He's big and strong and does the backbreaking work of the farm all by himself. True, he has a temper, and isn't afraid to use the whip when you've been bad. But that's not very often, because John Proctor is the kind of man who makes you *want* to do what he asks. And when he praises you, it's like God Himself reached down from heaven and ruffled your hair. Maybe best of all, he knows how to make you laugh—he may be strict, but he's no sourpuss.

In the community of Salem, John Proctor is important, not for what he is—he's just a farmer—but for *who* he is. No one is more generous in helping his neighbors, and no one is more honest in his dealings. If he has a fault, it's that he's too honest: when he thinks you're wrong, he'll tell you to your face, even in front of other people. Anyone on the receiving end of such blunt criticism is bound to resent it. And John Proctor has made some enemies in Salem by his plain speaking. Reverend Parris is one.

But maybe if Proctor hadn't been so admirable, he wouldn't be in the mess he's in. Abigail Williams fell in love with John Proctor's strength and honesty. What young woman wouldn't see him as the man of her dreams? His wife was sick, he was lonely, and he made the perfectly human mistake of succumbing to Abigail's adoration. But he made an even bigger mistake, as far as Abigail is concerned, when he rejected her and went back to his wife. As the saying goes, "Hell hath no fury like a woman scorned," and Abigail pays him back with a vengeance.

Elizabeth Proctor must have fallen for John just as hard as Abigail did. But Elizabeth seems almost afraid of her feelings, and doesn't express them easily. Her husband's passion and sexuality no doubt frightened her, and he probably felt rebuffed and disappointed when she didn't—or couldn't—return his ardent expressions of love. Then after his affair with Abigail, he not only felt guilty but shamed by Elizabeth's self-control. She says, "I never thought you but a good man, John—only somewhat bewildered." How can he believe such meekness? If their positions were reversed, he'd have torn her limb from limb.

John Proctor is not the same man to himself as he is to others. In a way, their admiration revolts him, because he is disgusted with himself. Elizabeth hints at his problem when she says, "The magistrate sits in your heart that judges you." And the judgment is harsh: John Proctor is a fraud. Before Abigail came along and ruined his peace, he was always sure of himself. He still is, but what he is sure of now is that nothing he can ever do will be pure and honest again.

In Christian doctrine, there is one sin for which there can be no forgiveness. It is called despair, and it means giving up hope because you're so bad not even God can forgive you. John Proctor is heading toward despair when the play begins, and he is pushed closer to the edge as the witch madness unfolds. In the end he finds his goodness and is saved, but it's a close call.

Elizabeth Proctor

The first we hear of Elizabeth Proctor is from Abigail Williams, who calls her a bitter, lying, cold, sniveling woman. Abigail has a tendency to blacken anyone who doesn't like her. But when we finally meet Elizabeth herself, she does seem pretty cool toward her husband, John. And if she's not exactly bitter about John's fling with Abigail, she isn't happy about it either. But who would be? She has a right to be jeal-

ous, and suspicious, too, especially when she finds
out that the last time John was in town he saw Abigail
alone—not in a crowd, as he had first told her. Elizabeth wants John to go back to the judges and expose
Abigail's lie about there being witchcraft in Salem, not
just to help the town, but to prove he's not still in love
with Abigail. When John loses his temper because he
can't stand being judged any more, Elizabeth stands
up to him:

> . . . you [will] come to know that I will be your
> only wife, or no wife at all!

Cold, suspicious, possessive: not an attractive picture
of Elizabeth Proctor. The question is, what was she
like *before* John "strayed"? Later on, when she sees
him for the last time before he's hanged, she answers
this question herself: "It needs a cold wife to prompt
lechery."

This painful honesty about herself brings out another quality in Elizabeth Proctor. Abigail calls her a
gossiping liar, but John thinks of her as "that goodness," and tells everyone that Elizabeth never told a
lie in her life. Indeed, according to her husband, Elizabeth *can't* lie. This sounds like an exaggeration, and
maybe John is making her out to be better than she is
because he himself feels so guilty about having betrayed her. He could also be bragging because he's
proud of her goodness.

When she does tell a lie, it is to save John's name:
she denies to the court that her husband was an adulterer. Ironically, this lie does the opposite of what she
intended, because John's already confessed—now it
looks like *he's* lying. As Reverend Hale says, it's a natural lie to tell, and even though it didn't work, it took

some courage for Elizabeth to lie to the most powerful authority in the province.

Courage has been defined as "being scared and doing it anyway." This describes Elizabeth's behavior when she is arrested. Although obviously scared to death, she promises to fear nothing. And then, as if to prove it, perhaps to herself as well as the others in the room, she says, "Tell the children I have gone to visit someone sick." This may be whistling in the dark—talking about everyday things to keep her fear from overwhelming her—but the fact that she can think of her children at a time like this is impressive.

But Elizabeth's courage is not blind—she's intelligent as well as brave. When she hears that her name has been "somewhat mentioned" in court, she realizes Abigail is out to get her. It won't be enough for John to talk to the court about Abigail; he will have to go to Abigail herself. From one tiny clue, Elizabeth figures out Abigail's whole monstrous plan to take her place with John. And she instantly knows what to do about it.

After her arrest, and all through her trial, Elizabeth refuses to confess to witchcraft, even though this lie would save her life. This is brave and noble. But as soon as she discovers she is pregnant, she doesn't hesitate to tell her jailers immediately, knowing that this fact will probably spare her, at least for a while.

And in the last act Elizabeth shows not only wisdom but great love for her husband when he is agonizing over whether to confess. He asks her what he should do. She knows he is so confused that he will probably do whatever she says. She desperately wants him alive, especially now that a baby's on the way. But she refuses to choose for him: "As you will, I would have it," leaving him free to decide his own destiny. But she does give him her blessing:

> Only be sure of this, for I know it now:
> Whatever you will do, it is a good man
> does it.

Abigail Williams

If there is a "bad guy" in *The Crucible*, Abigail Williams is it. She is the one who first led the girls to Tituba for dancing in the woods and conjuring spirits. When Tituba is forced to "confess," Abigail jumps right in and the other girls follow her. During the witch trials she is the girls' leader, bringing them into the court and presiding over their "torments." She intimidates everyone—the girls, the townsfolk, even the judges. And then, when it begins to look as if the tide is turning against her, she gets out while the getting is good, robbing her uncle, Reverend Parris, before she goes.

Abigail is a lot like the little girl in the movie *The Bad Seed*. In the movie, a nine-year-old terrorizes her family and the whole community. She murders several people, including her parents. She gets away with it because no one can believe that a child could be so evil. Anyone who *does* find her out, she kills.

Abigail lies without shame, threatens without fear, and thinks of nothing of sticking a needle two inches into her own belly in order to bring about the murder of Elizabeth Proctor. And she gets away with most of it.

But Abigail isn't a child. She's had a grown-up love affair with John Proctor, and has lost her childish faith in "the lying lessons I was taught by all these Christian women and their covenanted men." A child, when hurt, may strike back in anger. But only an adult could so coolly plot and execute the ingenious revenge Abigail plans for Elizabeth.

The important thing to decide about Abigail is whether you think she's evil or not. Without doubt, almost all her actions have evil consequences, and if there is good in her, we don't get to see much of it. She takes the lead in "crying out" witches; the other girls take their cues from her. In a very short time she has the whole town at her mercy, and she uses this power unscrupulously. In fact, a real witch could hardly have done a better job of destroying the community.

But is Abigail the only one to blame? If so, then what happened in Salem was a fluke, a case of one bad apple spoiling the barrel. Everyone else is therefore innocent; they just happened to be in the wrong place at the wrong time.

One thing that supports this idea is an old convention of writing plays that goes back to the Middle Ages. Certain plays called "moralities" always had a stock character called the Vice. The Vice was a troublemaker; his whole purpose was to stir things up, to set characters against each other, and to try to destroy the established order of things. Often the Vice was the Devil in disguise, but since these plays were put on by the church, he always lost in the end, most of the time by getting caught in one of his own traps. Abigail certainly fits this description, except for the last item— she doesn't get caught.

But some believe that considering Abigail the "bad guy" misses Arthur Miller's point. These people think that the real "bad guy" in *The Crucible* is superstition. With or without Abigail, there'd have been no witch madness if there'd been no *belief* in witches. If you look at it this way, Abigail, although you'd hardly call her innocent, is not entirely to blame either. Other girls cry out witches too; and it looks as if they were prompted, not by Abigail, but by their parents. If Abigail is evil, she's not alone. The madness itself, caused by superstition, is to blame. One person alone could never wreak such havoc.

But however you think of her, Abigail Williams is a fascinating character. We see her only twice—in Act I and Act III—but her presence and her influence dominate the whole play.

Mary Warren

Poor Mary Warren! When we first meet her briefly in Act I, she's afraid of everything. She was afraid to dance with the other girls in the woods. Now that the girls have been caught, she's afraid she'll be hanged as a witch, if Abigail doesn't tell the whole truth. Most of all she's afraid of Abigail—until John Proctor comes in and scares her back home.

But in Act II, when Proctor calls Mary a mouse, Elizabeth corrects him: "It is a mouse no more." Now that Mary's an official of the court, she can stand up even to John Proctor's rage. Has Mary Warren suddenly become brave? Of course not. Her courage comes from the court, from being one of the group.

And in Act III, not even John Proctor's great strength can keep her from breaking under the stress of being "cried out" by Abigail and the other girls. Mary's more afraid of Abigail than anything, even the fact that "God damns all liars," and this fear finally overwhelms her.

Is this a totally spineless creature? Probably not. Few people could stand up under the ordeal that Mary Warren is put through in Act III, and it's a wonder she holds out as long as she does. Considering how easily frightened Mary is by nature, she shows tremendous courage in coming to the court at all. True, Proctor is making her do it; but once the ordeal has begun, Mary holds her own against Abigail longer than anybody. But when Proctor is discredited, she loses his support; and when even the judges turn against her, Mary finally breaks.

Mary can hardly be called evil. She tells the truth, unless she is intimidated into doing otherwise. She makes the poppet as a gift for Elizabeth. Maybe Mary does this to make up for being away from her chores for so long, but maybe this is the action of a kind heart as well as a guilty conscience.

Above all, Mary's naïve: she's slow to believe evil of anyone. Perhaps this is why she cannot resist the evil that overwhelms her—she didn't know how strong it was because she didn't know it was there in the first place.

And could it also be loneliness that draws Mary Warren into this catastrophe? Out on Proctor's farm, John and Elizabeth have each other and the children for companionship—they are a family. Mary is an orphan, an outsider, living on the Proctor's charity. Three times she disobeys Proctor's orders and sneaks into town: once to watch the other girls dance, again the next day "to see the great doings in the world," and finally to go to court as an "official." Is it excitement she's after? In part, perhaps, but in town she is a member of a group; at home, she is just a lone servant. Maybe what crushes her in Act III is not just the harshness of the judges and the hysteria of her friends, but her isolation. She's not afraid to tell the truth, she's afraid to stand alone.

Reverend John Hale

Arthur Miller describes Reverend Hale as "nearing forty, a tight-skinned, eager-eyed intellectual." An intellectual is usually thought of as someone with his head in the clouds, who spends so much time thinking great thoughts that he's inept in the real world of human emotions. There is some truth in this image of John Hale. He knows a lot about witchcraft; but he knows almost nothing about the people of Salem or the "contention" that is wracking the town. How pompous and arrogant he must sound when he says, "Have no fear now—we shall find [the Devil] out if he has come among us, and I mean to crush him utterly if he has shown his face!"

And yet he has every reason to be confident. To Hale, demonology is an exact science, for he has spent his whole life in the study of it. But he is not just a bookworm, he is a minister of God. "His goal is light, goodness and its preservation," and he is excited by being "called upon to face what may be a bloody fight with the Fiend himself." All his years of preparation may now finally be put to the test.

He fails, and the evil that follows his first appearance totally overwhelms him. Why? Is the fault in his character? Is he not as smart as he thinks he is? Is he a fool, whose meddling lit the fuse to the bomb that blew up the town? Some say yes, and much of the play supports this answer. What looks like success at the end of Act I soon carries Hale out of his depth, and each time he appears after that he is less sure of himself. At the end of the play he has been completely crushed: he, a minister of the light, has "come to do the Devil's work. I come to counsel Christians they should belie themselves. There is blood on my head! Can you not see the blood on my head!!"

It's hard to imagine going through a more horrifying experience than the disillusionment of the Reverend Mr. Hale. All those years of dedicated, loving study made worthless by a band of hysterical and not-at-all innocent girls. Made worse than worthless—his learning ends up sending nineteen people to the gallows. And worst of all, he is helpless to stop it, having started it in the first place.

Is there evil in this man? Perhaps. According to Christian doctrine, one of the seven deadly (or damnable) sins is pride. In a way it's the worst one, because it was pride that made the devil rebel against God. And Reverend Hale, when he first appears, feels "the pride of the specialist whose unique knowledge has at last been publicly called for."

He certainly gets his comeuppance.

Reverend Samuel Parris

At the beginning of the play, when his little girl Betty lies sick on her bed, Reverend Parris is less worried about her condition than about what the neighbors will think if it turns out Betty is "witched." Like a lot of selfish people, he feels persecuted: anyone who disagrees with Reverend Parris is his enemy, part of a conspiracy that's out to "get him." He is convinced that John Proctor is the leader of this conspiracy, because Proctor's always criticizing him. Proctor doesn't come to church anymore because, as he says, Reverend Parris can talk of nothing but hell and damnation—"Take it to heart, Mr. Parris. There are many others who stay away from church these days because you hardly ever mention God any more."

Parris also seems to be greedy. Proctor tells Reverend Hale in Act II that Parris can't "pray to God without he have golden candlesticks upon the altar." Parris claims that in addition to his salary Salem owes him money for firewood, and he wants the deed to his house—two things no minister had demanded before.

Parris is unhappy in Salem, and maybe he has his reasons. He says at one point, "I cannot offer one proposition without there be a howling riot of argument." In the past few years, two ministers had left Salem in disgust with the town's contentiousness and stinginess. Thomas Putnam had even had one of them, George Burroughs, put in jail for debts he did not owe. On top of that, Parris is a Harvard graduate, which his predecessors were not, so he feels he deserves more than the town is willing to give.

Whatever the reasons for his discontent, Reverend Parris doesn't seem to be a very nice person anyway. He bullies and mistreats his servant Tituba, and tries to do the same with Abigail. But he flatters and fawns on those in power, such as Thomas Putnam and Danforth. With everyone else he is arrogant and sometimes downright insulting.

Almost every time he opens his mouth it is to attack someone. When the court is first set up, he hides behind it like a child behind a parent, and he loses no chance to set the court against his "enemies," especially John Proctor. When Francis Nurse presents the court with a petition in favor of his wife Rebecca, it is Parris' idea that the 91 people who signed the petition should be arrested. As long as the court is in power, Parris is its staunchest support. But in Act IV, when the town is beginning to turn against the court, Parris is the first to look for a way out.

Imagine his horror when Abigail disappears at the end of the play. The court has lost its star witness, the leader of the girls on whose testimony all the witches have been hanged. Parris himself has lost a niece, but worst of all, Abigail robbed his strongbox before she left, and now he's penniless. As Salem's pastor, he should have protected his flock. Not only did he let the wolves into the fold, he joined in the attack. Now the wolves are in trouble, and Parris is left without a friend in the world.

It's hard to feel sorry for the Reverend Samuel Parris. But there is something pathetic about a man who is so insecure that he has to persecute others to save his own skin.

Deputy Governor Danforth

Overall, Deputy Governor Danforth does more damage in this play than anyone else, even Abigail Williams. As Deputy Governor of Massachusetts, he is the second most powerful man in the province. As head of the court, he has the authority to try, convict, and execute anyone he sees fit. Abigail may "cry out" innocent people as witches; Danforth hangs them.

Some would say he is a rigid man, especially in his sticking to the letter of the law. In Act III he will not let Giles Corey submit his evidence unless it is in proper affidavit form. In Act IV, unless John Proctor will sign a written confession, it is no confession. In everything he does, Danforth is most concerned with staying within the precise limits of the statutes.

But look at what he's faced with. To him "there is a moving plot to topple Christ in the country," and he is willing to use every ounce of his prodigious power to prevent that from happening. If he gives in the slightest bit, God's whole defensive line will break. Considering the way he sees the situation, it takes tremendous strength and courage to stand so firm against such a formidable attack.

And don't forget that to the Puritans the law, with which Danforth seems so obsessed, was made not by man but by God. Massachusetts at this time is a theocracy—a government ordained by God as his "visible Kingdome" on Earth. Reverend Hale is thinking exactly like Danforth when he tells Proctor in Act II:

> Theology [literally, "God's word"], sir,
> is a fortress; no crack in a fortress may
> be accounted small.

Even bending the law a little is dangerous business, especially at such a dangerous time as this.

Ironically, it is Danforth's strength and courage that allow the witch madness to grow to such monstrous proportions. A weaker man would have broken under the strain; a man less brave would have quailed before hanging someone like Rebecca Nurse. Under a shakier hand, the court's authority might have disintegrated, and after some confusion, life would have returned to normal.

But for all his rigidity, there seems to be no malice in Danforth, as there is in Parris and Hathorne. His intentions are good, heroic, even. He just happens to be wrong. And nineteen innocent people are hanged on his signature.

Rebecca Nurse

Although she appears only twice in *The Crucible*, Rebecca Nurse is important to everyone else in the play. Her reputation in Salem is so high that when she's first accused of witchcraft, hardly anyone can believe it. To Reverend Hale, "if Rebecca Nurse be tainted, then nothing's left to stop the whole green world from burning." To those like Proctor who don't believe in witchcraft, Rebecca's being "cried out" is the most monstrous lie imaginable. To the witch-hunters, she's a great catch.

Rebecca is perhaps less a "person" than a symbol of sanity in a world that's lost its mind. She retains her dignity and courage to the very end. When asked one last time if she will confess, she says, "Why, it is a lie, it is a lie; how may I damn myself? I cannot, I cannot."

But her answer may express something else besides courage. She's an old woman, close to her end anyway. Her life so far has been blameless, why spoil it now? It's not common sense.

Perhaps this sensible attitude helps her keep her humor as well. Her last line, spoken as she almost collapses on her way out to be hanged, is, "I've had no breakfast."

Giles Corey

Giles Corey is superstitious about his wife's reading books, and he's forever taking his neighbors to court on the smallest excuse. He's afraid of no one, and has a sharp tongue for anybody who thinks he can be made a fool of. But he makes a fool of himself by being so ready to scrap all the time. He's 83, and set in his ways. In any other play he'd be a comic figure: the stock character of the crotchety old man. But this play is not a comedy, and for all his comic characteristics, Giles Corey is destroyed along with all the other victims of the witch madness.

Giles is more than a stubborn old geezer. Life was extremely hard in those days. Just to be alive at age 83 was in itself a remarkable achievement. But Giles shows little sign of running out of steam: John Proctor thinks nothing of asking Giles' help in dragging his lumber home.

Is Giles as bull-headed as he at first appears? Before he married Martha, his third wife (he buried the other two), he had little time for church. But now he's learned his commandments and makes a serious effort to pray. In Act I he passes up a perfect chance to twit his hated neighbor Thomas Putnam—Putnam claims that Proctor's lumber belongs to him—and instead stays to hear what the learned Reverend Hale has to say. Giles may be slow to change his mind, but he's not against learning something new.

But just because he's slow, it doesn't mean he's dumb. He may never understand the subtleties of demonology, but "thirty-three time in court" has taught Giles Corey how to recognize greed when he sees it. And he knows enough about the law to keep silent when he is formally charged with witchcraft. By not answering the indictment, he dies a good Christian under the law, and the court cannot confiscate his property, as it did with the other "witches." In this way his sons inherit, and he keeps his land out of Putnam's clutches.

In the end, the way he dies tells the most about him:

> Great stones they lay upon his chest until
> he plead aye or nay. They say he give them
> but two words. "More weight," he says.
> And died.

As Elizabeth Proctor says, "It were a fearsome man, Giles Corey."

Other Elements

SETTING

The Crucible is set in the small settlement of Salem, Massachusetts, in 1692. The first three acts take place in the spring, and the fourth act in the fall.

Actually there were two Salems—Salem Town and its tiny suburb, Salem Village. Reverend Parris' house was in Salem Village, and it was here that his slave Tituba, his daughter Betty, and his niece Abigail Williams first "came down with" witchcraft. The trials, however, were held for the most part in the large meeting house in Salem Town.

Each act is set within a fairly small room: Act I is in a bedroom in Reverend Parris' house; Act II in the Proctors' "living room"; Act III in an anteroom to the main hall of the "meeting house," or church; and Act IV in a cell in the Salem jail. These settings give an impression of containment, almost of claustrophobia, as if we're boxed in, caught in a trap. As the pressure builds in each act, a sense of panic is bound to set in. Of course, this is exactly what the victims of the witch-hunt must be feeling. Arthur Miller's settings help us identify with the characters, by putting us, in a sense, in the same room with them.

THEMES

A number of thematic threads run through *The Crucible*. Some of them contradict others, some of them overlap. And no one of them completely explains the play. You'll find that some of them ring more true to you than others, but you can find evidence to support all of them in the play. These themes are:

1. A SOCIAL DRAMA

Arthur Miller is dramatizing a bizarre but not uncommon social phenomenon. The explanation for the witch madness can be found in the makeup of the society itself. The play was written at a time when American society was threatened by a similar madness, over communism instead of witchcraft. The author is telling us that it might happen again, and we'd better do something about it.

2. A PERSONAL TRAGEDY

The Crucible is really about one man's struggle with his conscience. The whole play revolves around John Proctor. The witch madness serves only to intensify and focus Proctor's energies on his problems with his wife, his neighbors, and himself.

3. HYSTERIA

The play demonstrates an outbreak of that peculiar insanity called mass hysteria. We get to see how easily reasonable human beings can become unhinged in an environment that allows little opportunity for letting off steam. Once the seal is broken on the pressure cooker, it explodes.

4. SUPERSTITION

There were no real witches in Salem. Without the superstitious belief in witchcraft, this catastrophe could never have happened. Arthur Miller blames "them that quail to bring men out of ignorance" for this tragedy, and is making a plea for a more enlightened approach to religious beliefs.

5. GREED AND VENGEANCE

Several characters find "monstrous profit" in the witch madness, and manipulate events for their own ends. Thomas Putnam, the richest man in town, acquires quite a bit of land by having his daughter Ruth "cry out" his neighbors. And Abigail Williams accomplishes a pretty sweet revenge on the Proctors when her affair with John is broken off.

6. AUTHORITY

This play examines the question of authority: who has the power, and on what is that power based? What is the proper use of authority, and what is abuse of power? The judges believe they derive their authority from God, and so carry on the witch-hunt as if they are on a holy mission. They're deceived by the girls, and refuse to believe the obvious truth when it's staring them in the face. What went wrong?

7. THEOCRACY

The separation of church and state, which is one of the cornerstones of the American Constitution, did not exist in seventeenth-century Massachusetts. "Theocracy" means "Government by God," and the Puritans believed that they were establishing God's "visible Kingdome" on earth—the state was to be governed by God's laws. But this mixing up of the laws of God and the laws of men led directly to the legal chaos of the Salem witch trials.

8. JUSTICE

The concept of justice is central to most of Arthur Miller's plays, especially The Crucible, where he dedicates the entire third act to a courtroom drama. How can we guarantee that a person accused of a crime gets a fair trial? And how should the guilty be punished?

9. HISTORICAL DRAMA

The Crucible tells a story of the American past, a time when many of the basic principles of our society were formed. It's possible, the playwright suggests, that some of the things that were wrong in 1692 are still wrong today.

STYLE

Plays can be classified in two major varieties: plays of episodic action and plays of continuous action. Shakespeare's plays are episodic. No one scene is very long, and the action jumps around from place to place, sometimes skipping over years in between. On the other hand, Greek tragedies like *Oedipus Rex* and some modern plays such as Eugene O'Neill's *Long Day's Journey into Night*, follow what are called the three unities: of *time*—the action usually takes place within a 24-hour period; of *place*—there is only one location; and of *action*—there is no break in the action from beginning to end.

The Crucible falls somewhere in between. The time span is about three-and-a-half months; the action occurs in four different places, although it never leaves Salem; and there is a gap of at least a week between each act (between Acts III and IV almost three months elapse). But within each act the action is continuous from curtain to curtain.

One advantage of the continuous-action method is that it allows the author to build tension or suspense gradually. It also can be less confusing for an audience, because we don't have to stop and figure out where we are every few minutes. And, finally, it allows us to get to know the main characters very well, by letting us watch them for a long time at a stretch. This is especially important in *The Crucible*, where we come to understand what happened in Salem in 1692 through the experience of one man, John Proctor.

Perhaps the most remarkable aspect of the style of *The Crucible* is its language. These people speak a dialect that is much closer to Shakespeare's English than to our own. Shakespeare's time was full of adventure and discovery, and his language reflected that excitement and energy.

The Puritans themselves were outspoken. One reason they were driven to the New World in the first place was that they couldn't keep quiet about religious matters. And most of them came from the lower classes, whose language is generally very earthy.

Add these things up, and then add in the rugged life these pioneers were forced to lead in the early years of American settlement, and you come up with a way of speaking that is sometimes called "muscular."

Arthur Miller has made his characters speak the way they think—bluntly, directly, and with little concern for fancy phrase-making. He took some lines straight out of writings of the time, including transcripts of the witch trials. The result is a kind of rough poetry, sometimes of great power.

POINT OF VIEW

Arthur Miller has chosen to tell the story of the Salem witch trials from the point of view of one of its victims, John Proctor. This personalizes the story for us; by the end we know Proctor better than anyone else in the play, and we feel his suffering all the more intensely because we care about him. We also come to understand what happens by following and sharing Proctor's struggle to understand it himself.

Proctor is an extremely attractive character. He is as good and honest as we ourselves would like to be, and yet he's not perfect. His mistakes are those of a human being, not a superman. By concentrating the action of the play on John Proctor, Arthur Miller makes it easy for us not only to sympathize, but also to identify with him and the other victims of the witch-hunt: we find out what it would *feel* like to be caught up in such madness.

FORM AND STRUCTURE

For the published version of *The Crucible*, Arthur Miller has inserted passages of prose in which he comments on the background of the story or the characters. These comments tell you a lot about Miller's thinking, but they interrupt the flow of the action, and you may want to skip them the first time you read the play. Then you can go back and read them all together, or pick them up along the way on your second read-through. You should always read a play twice: you'll be amazed how much you missed the first time, and how much more sense it makes the second time around when you know what's going to happen next.

The Crucible has a lot of characters, 21 speaking parts in all, plus quite a few people who are talked about but never appear onstage, like Ruth Putnam and Martha Corey. Each of these characters has a story to tell, and every story is important. It's easy to become lost unless you can see how each subplot ties into and advances the main plot, which is the flareup of witch panic in Salem.

The story is indeed complicated, but Arthur Miller makes it easier to follow by the way he has designed the play. He begins each act by setting up a terrible possibility, and ends each act by bringing that terrible thing to pass.

In Act I the question is: "Will the town leap to witchcraft?" The curtain falls on Tituba, Abigail, and Betty ecstatically "crying out witches."

In Act II the question is: "Will the Proctors get caught up by the witch-hunt?" The act ends with Elizabeth Proctor being led away in chains.

In Act III the question is: "Will Abigail foil John Proctor's attempt to discredit her?" The answer is, yes, and more, for Proctor himself is arrested as a witch.

Then in Act IV the question is: "Will John Proctor hang?" He does.

This repeated pattern of question and answer—"Will the worst happen?" "Yes."—is the rhythm of the play. You can think of what happens between the setup and the payoff in each act as a kind of tug-of-war: some characters pull toward catastrophe, others pull away from it, and invariably the first group overpowers the second. If you think about the action in terms of this tug-of-war, the plot will be a lot easier to follow.

SOME NOTES ON READING THE PLAY

There's a difference between reading a play and reading a novel. The most obvious thing is that a play is all dialogue, whereas a novel will often have many paragraphs of prose describing what a character is thinking. In a play you have to figure out what a character is thinking by what he says, and what others say about him, keeping in mind that people don't always speak the truth, or at least the whole truth.

Another difference between a novel and a play is the audience each is intended for. When a novel appears in print, it is as ready as it's going to be for its audience, the individual reader. But the script of a play is a blueprint for a performance by actors, in makeup and costume, on a stage set, before an audience of more than one. Whatever ideas a playwright has in mind, whatever words he puts on paper, the play is meant to be seen and heard, not just read silently by one person slouching in an armchair.

But even if you can't actually attend a performance, and have to settle for reading the script, there is a way to get a more complete idea of what the play's supposed to be. Read some of it aloud, "playing" the different characters: How would you say these words if you were in the same situation? What gesture would you use to make this point? Maybe you can get a friend to try it with you. It may sound silly or embarrassing, but it really does help. And it's fun.

The Story

Although the action is continuous in each act of *The Crucible*, this guide breaks the acts into what are called "French scenes." A new French scene begins every time a major character enters or exits.

ACT I

ACT I, SCENE 1

From the moment the curtain rises, we know something is wrong. A little girl, Betty Parris, lies inert on the bed. What's the matter with her? Is she sick? Hurt? Her father, Reverend Samuel Parris, is weeping and praying frantically over her. The next three things that happen tell us things are really bad: 1) the black slave Tituba, obviously very frightened, comes in begging Parris to tell her that her Betty's "not goin' to die," and Parris furiously drives her out; 2) Betty's cousin Abigail Williams comes in to announce a message from Dr. Griggs, which means that Betty's been like this for some time; and 3) Susanna Walcott delivers the doctor's message: he cannot help Betty, so her affliction must be from "unnatural things," meaning witchcraft.

Parris' first reaction is to deny that Betty's "witched," which seems natural: it's a horrifying thought. Horrifying, but not out of the question, because Reverend Hale, a witchcraft expert from Beverly, has already been sent for and is on his way. Both Parris and Abigail warn Susanna to "speak nothin' of it in the village" on her way back to the doctor. This seems natural, too: Parris is trying to avoid panic among his congregation.

But we soon discover that Parris is more worried about his position in the village than he is about his daughter's health. Throughout the following interrogation, during which Abigail admits that she, Betty, and Tituba were dancing in the woods, Parris mentions his enemies four times, saying clearly at one point, "There is a faction that is sworn to drive me from my pulpit. Do you understand that?" In other words, the worst part of this scandal is that it began in his own house, a fact his enemies will surely take advantage of. For the rest of the play, Parris is consistent in his self-centeredness. No matter what happens to anybody else, he will always be concerned only about himself.

For her part, Abigail at first appears to be humble and repentant. She confesses that they danced, and she's willing to be whipped for it, even if they did it just for "sport." But Parris, in his anxiety about his own reputation, insinuates that Abigail's name is not "entirely white" in the town. Goodwife Proctor, it is said, "comes so rarely to the church this year for she will not sit so close to something soiled," meaning Abigail, who used to work as the Proctors' servant.

Abigail tells us a lot: instead of answering the accusation, she attacks the accuser. She says Goody Proctor hates her because Abigail would not be her slave; twice she calls Goody Proctor a liar. (Elizabeth Proctor's truthfulness will be very important later.) Abigail then turns her wrath on Parris: "Do you begrudge my bed, uncle?" (Later on, in Act II, Abigail will once again be accused of wrongdoing, and she will get out of it in exactly the same way.)

ACT I, SCENE 2

Parris has no chance to recover from this onslaught, for now the Putnams, Ann and then Thomas, come in, full of news. Their daughter Ruth has been stricken as well, and they are certain it's from "the Devil's touch." Parris' manner changes abruptly: with Tituba and Abigail he was sharp and angry, but now he seems most anxious to please. The Putnams must be important people, and we soon find out why. When Parris pleads with them, "leap not to witchcraft. . . . They will howl me out of Salem for such corruption in my house," Thomas Putnam replies, "Mr. Parris, I have taken your part in all contention here, and I would continue." Putnam is the minister's ally, and as such has power over him. Putnam will use his power to get his way in this matter, as we shall see.

Goody Putnam then explains how she knows this is witchcraft. Last night she sent Ruth to Tituba to contact the spirits of Ruth's seven baby brothers and sisters, all of whom had died—"murdered," according to their mother—before they were a day old.

'It is a formidable sin to conjure up the dead!" Parris cries, and turns in horror to Abigail. Of course, *she* had nothing to do with conjuring spirits: "Not I, sir— Tituba and Ruth." Once again, all Parris can think of is himself: "Oh, Abigail, what proper payment for my charity! Now I am undone." But Thomas Putnam has a plan. If Parris will quit dithering and take charge of the situation, he will not be undone. "Let you strike out against the Devil, and the village will bless you for it!" Parris, swayed by this argument—which not only makes sense, but also flatters his self-important image of himself—goes down to the parlor with the Putnams to lead the people in a psalm.

I said that Putnam's argument made sense, and it does, but only if you accept the premise that Betty and Ruth are in fact "witched." And this has not yet been proven even to Parris's satisfaction. But Putnam puts it to him in such a way that the only thing Parris can do to save himself is to "Wait for no one to charge you—declare it [witchcraft] yourself." And Parris, being who he is, has to go along. Whatever his doubts, whatever his fears, his actions say, "This is witchcraft."

NOTE: Every act is studded with such moments, seemingly innocent or unavoidable decisions that determine the direction of future events. Here Parris takes the first small step toward the horror that will follow.

And a word here about "proof." It is the most troublesome issue in the play: how do you *prove* witchcraft? Everyone seems to have a different answer. Look at Goody Putnam's speech, "They were murdered, Mr. Parris! And mark this proof! Mark it! Last night my Ruth were ever so little close to their little spirits; I know it, sir. For how else is she struck dumb now except some power of darkness would stop her mouth? It is a marvelous sign, Mr. Parris!" Later on Reverend Hale, the expert on witchcraft, will say, "We cannot look to superstition in this. The Devil is precise." But the question of what constitutes proof of witchcraft and what is mere superstition is never resolved in the play, and Arthur Miller is almost totally silent about it. So we too will have to reserve judgment, and just take note of these "proofs" as they are presented.

ACT I, SCENE 3

Just before they leave, the Putnams' maidservant Mercy Lewis comes in with further word on Ruth's condition: "She give a powerful sneeze . . . another like it will shake her wits together, I'm sure." This sounds like good news, and for a moment it looks as if the trouble might clear up by itself.

As soon as the grownups are gone, Abigail becomes all business. They've got to get their stories straight: they're in trouble for sure, but if they're careful they can keep it from getting worse. Mary Warren, the Proctor's maidservant, runs in in a panic, ready to blab everything. Mercy and Abigail close in on her menacingly, when suddenly little Betty wakes up. Abigail tries to soothe her, but Betty streaks for the window, crying out for her dead mama. And at last we find out what Abigail was really up to last night. "You drank blood, Abby!" Betty cries. "You drank a charm to kill John Proctor's wife!" Abigail smashes her across the face to shut her up, and makes a naked threat to the other two:

Let either of you breathe a word, or the edge of a word . . . and I will come to you in the black of some terrible night and I will bring a pointy reckoning that will shudder you. And you know I can do it; I saw Indians smash my dear parents' heads on the pillow next to mine, and I have seen some reddish work done at night, and I can make you wish you had never seen the sun go down!

If any shred of innocence has clung to Abigail up until this point, it now is vaporized. It's possible she's just scared and is trying to scare the others into keeping quiet. It's also possible she drank the charm against Goody Proctor "for sport." But even if that's true, it's pretty nasty sport. Whether you believe she means her threat or not, it's clear that Abigail Williams is a dangerous person. In fact, if anybody in the play talks like a witch, it's Abigail. Soon she'll do far worse.

ACT I, SCENE 4

John Proctor enters, looking for Mary Warren. His appearance startles the girls, and Mary and Mercy Lewis quickly scurry out. Betty has relapsed into lifelessness, so Proctor and Abigail are in effect alone. At once we are aware that these two know each other well, perhaps better than they should. They speak with an easy familiarity, and smile as if they share a secret. He's heard rumors of witchcraft in the town. "Oh, posh!" Abigail replies. "We were dancin' in the woods last night, and my uncle leaped in on us. She [Betty] took fright, is all." How many faces does this Abigail have? We've now heard three different versions of her story; which one are we to believe? Proctor seems to know: his smile widens as he says, "Ah, you're wicked yet, aren't y'! You'll be clapped in the stocks before you're twenty."

But Abigail wants more from him than casual banter. "Give me a word, John. A soft word." His answer, "No, no, Abby. That's done with," tells us that the rumor is true, something *did* happen to cause Goody Proctor to put Abigail out of the house. But for Abby it's definitely *not* done with. For the rest of the scene she tries to get Proctor to admit he still loves her. And although he keeps repeating that it's over between them, he never actually says, "I don't love you any more."

Suddenly, a whole new dimension of the play opens up. Before this scene, the situation has looked like not much more than a prank that backfired. The girls were just letting off steam, and the adults are taking the whole thing too seriously. Indeed, when Rebecca Nurse enters a few moments later, that is her explanation for the whole affair. For the rest of the girls this may be true, but for Abigail there's more at stake. We have seen the dark passion that flows between her and John Proctor, and we know her too well by now to believe that she'll let this thing rest. Not if she can use it to get what she wants.

NOTE: What is this "heat" between Abigail and Proctor? Is it true love, or is it just the lust of the flesh? Or maybe some of both? At this point it's hard to tell. Abigail remembers "how you clutched my back behind your house and sweated like a stallion whenever I come near!" This sure sounds like lust. But later, in tears, she pleads with him: "I look for John Proctor who took me from my sleep and put knowledge in my heart! I never knew what pretense Salem was, I never knew the lying lessons I was taught by all these Christian women and their covenanted men! And now you bid me tear the light out of my eyes? I will not, I cannot! You loved me, John Proctor, and what-

ever sin it is, you love me yet! John, pity me, pity me!"
The earnestness of such a speech is hard to doubt.

As for Proctor, we hardly know him yet, but compared to the others we have met so far, he seems the
opposite: honest, even when it hurts him; determined
to do the right thing, even though it makes him and
others suffer. We will have more of a chance to exam-
ine his heart later, for he will soon emerge as the hero
of this tragedy. For the moment, however, let's just
take note of how intense their feelings are for each
other, and watch for further developments.

ACT I, SCENE 5

A psalm is being sung below, and suddenly Betty
starts screaming. Her father rushes in, followed by the
Putnams, Rebecca Nurse, and an old farmer named
Giles Corey. Parris is terrified: it seems as if Betty cannot bear to hear the Lord's name. The rest look on
with curiosity, all of them believing this to be a "prodigious sign" that witchcraft is afoot. All except
Rebecca Nurse. She goes over and merely stands
beside the bed, which miraculously calms Betty
down. Once again it seems as if the whole thing might
just blow over, and for a moment everything is
calm.

But the Putnams are not convinced by Rebecca's
soothing explanations. They don't believe it's God's
will that all Rebecca's children should survive, while
all of their own wither on the night of their birth. John
Proctor sides with Rebecca, and wants to know why
Parris sent for Reverend Hale before calling a town
meeting. At this point, a full-blown squabble breaks
out, and we get to see at first hand the "contention" in
the town that Reverend Parris complained about in
the first scene. Proctor won't come to church because

Parris hardly mentions God anymore. Parris wants the congregation to give him money for firewood, as well as a deed to his house. And everybody argues over who owns what land.

NOTE: As we saw in The Author and His Times section of this guide, land was already a sore point with the Puritans of Salem. Arthur Miller brings it up here because it will play such a horrible part in the nightmare to come. We will find out that Thomas Putnam in particular stands to gain quite a bit by having his neighbors cried out as witches. And we will also see Giles Corey, who seems like such a comical character now, go to incredible lengths to keep his land from being taken from him. The question of witchcraft will be inseparable from the question of land ownership from beginning to end.

ACT I, SCENE 6

Into this melee comes Reverend John Hale, "loaded down with half a dozen heavy books."

NOTE: The books may seem to be just a device, a nice touch to round out Reverend Hale's character, like a pair of glasses, or ink on his hands. But in a way the books are more important than the man who carries them. Reverend Hale is an expert on witchcraft, but his expertise comes from the books. They are heavy, "weighted with authority." Without them, Reverend Hale would be no better than the others, a man with an opinion. If the others look to him for answers, he looks to the books. It is on the books' "authority" that the witches will later be hanged.

But before he can begin even to find out if there *are* witches in this case, a disturbing thing happens. John Proctor, who *knows* the girls were only fooling around (he doesn't seem to have heard about the charm to kill his wife), leaves. Maybe he's giving up on what he sees as the foolishness of his neighbors, maybe he believes Reverend Hale will talk some sense into them. Shortly afterward, Rebecca Nurse follows Proctor out, saying she is "too old for this." She doesn't believe there is witchcraft here, and she also seems to be afraid that Reverend Hale's being here is a bad idea. There is no one left in the room who doubts the existence of witchcraft. Except maybe Abigail, but she is, as we have seen, a special case.

What follows is the logical result of removing the only really reasonable people from the scene. Had they stayed, they would certainly have hampered Mr. Hale's work, and the momentum that carries the town into witch madness might never have built up. To use the analogy of a tug-of-war, they let go of the rope.

Since the opening of the play we have been prepared for this moment; we have seen it coming. We expect to see some witchcraft. And Arthur Miller does not disappoint us.

The people in the room are all breathless, waiting for Mr. Hale and his books to work their magic. They all know that what takes place in the next few moments will probably change their lives. Even if he comes up with nothing, as he warns them might happen, and finds "no bruise of hell" on Betty, at least they will have witnessed a prodigious demonstration of deep learning.

But Hale has given them reason to hope for something more spectacular. This man has acquaintance with all familiar spirits—"your incubi and succubi;

your witches that go by land, by air, and by sea; your wizards of the night and of the day." He has promised that "If [Betty] is truly in the Devil's grip we may have to rip and tear to get her free." And as he is about to start, he warns them solemnly; "Now mark me, if the Devil is in her you will witness some frightful wonders in this room, so please keep your wits about you. Mr. Putnam, stand close in case she flies." Given the charged atmosphere in the room, if the Devil himself came up through the floor, it would hardly be unexpected. What Mr. Hale has in fact done is made it impossible for something *not* to happen.

He tries talking to Betty. Nothing. He asks if someone afflicts her, or some thing—"a pig, a mouse, or any beast at all." Nothing. He intones Latin over her: In the name of the Father and the Son, I bid you [who are afflicting this child] return to Hell! Nothing. He turns to Abigail. She squirms beneath his questions. Yes, they were dancing. Yes, there was a kettle of soup, but the live frog "jumped in, we never put it in!" Hale is on the scent now, and he bears down on her. "Did you call the Devil last night?"

Abigail has to get out of this. "I never called him! Tituba, Tituba . . ." and we're off. Now Abigail can confess everything because Tituba made her do it: made her drink blood, made her laugh at prayer, made her dream corruptions and stand "in the open doorway and not a stitch upon my body!" What answer can poor Tituba make to such a deluge of accusations? "No I didn't"? Who's going to believe that? On the contrary, the witch has been found.

Tituba's in a terrible jam. When she denies the charge that she compacted with the Devil, her master threatens to whip her to death, and Mr. Putnam adds that she must be hanged if she will not confess. Very

well, she'll confess. If you had to choose between a
noose and a false confession, which would you
choose? (Remember your answer for later.)

But to Tituba, it may not have been such a lie. The
Devil is real to these people. If they haven't seen him
"in the flesh," he is an active figure in their imagina-
tions. He is the Author of all Temptations, the Father
of Lies. And so, if a good Christian sins, it must be
because, in some way, "the Devil made him do it."

The point here is that Hale and the others lead Tituba into her confession by giving her nowhere else to
turn. And once she starts, the emotion of releasing
pent-up guilt and anger is so powerful that it sucks
Abigail and then Betty into its vortex. Witchcraft has
been revealed.

NOTE: But is the witchcraft real? Or are the girls
and Tituba "pretending," as Mary Warren will later
say? Modern psychology explains what happened in
Salem in 1692 as a case of "mass hysteria." Hysteria
often occurs when a person can't or won't express
powerful emotions—rage, say, or fear—which then
find an outlet in bizarre forms of behavior: outbursts
of laughter or fits of weeping for no apparent reason,
paralysis of the limbs for which no physical cause can
be found, sometimes dancing or trying to fly. And
hysteria can be contagious, especially in communities
with strongly shared values and strict codes of con-
duct. To those who "catch it," the affliction is completely real, they simply cannot control themselves.

But is hysteria the case here? Let's look at two strik-
ing moments in this climactic scene to see if we can get
a clue. The first happens during Tituba's "confession." Hale and Parris are pressing her for the names

of the people she's seen with the Devil. Instead of giving these names right away, she bursts out, "in a fury:"

> He say Mr. Parris must be kill! . . . Mr. Parris mean man and no gentle man, and he bid me rise out of my bed and cut your throat!

This is a violent non sequitur and, as such things often do, it tells us a lot of what Tituba *really* feels about her master.

There are three possible explanations for this outburst: 1) Tituba is being sly—she hates her master and sees this as a chance to get back at him; 2) Tituba has fantasized killing Parris, especially when he mistreated her, but she can't admit this to herself and blames it on the Devil; 3) The Devil actually came to her as she says, that is, Tituba, who has a vivid imagination, really believes what she's saying. The author leaves the choice up to us. What is clear is that all the people in the room take Tituba's statements as fact.

All of them, that is, with the possible exception of Abigail Williams. Throughout Tituba's confession Abby has remained silent. Suddenly she rises, "staring as though inspired," and cries out:

> I want to open myself! I want the light of God, I want the sweet love of Jesus! I danced for the Devil; I saw him; I wrote in his book; I go back to Jesus; I kiss His hand. I saw Sarah Good with the Devil! I saw Goody Osburn with the Devil! I saw Bridget Bishop with the Devil!

What are we to make of this? In this case we have a lot more to go on than we did with Tituba. Abigail's been on stage since the beginning of the act; by now we know her better than anyone else. We've seen her change her story for each new person she's told it to, we've seen her consistently shift blame onto others, we've heard her threaten the other girls with "a pointy reckoning," and we know she hates Goody Proctor. It's doubtful that she actually saw the Devil: earlier, when Proctor said the town's "mumbling witchcraft," her response was a contemptuous, "Oh, posh!"

But throughout this scene Tituba's been getting all the attention, and maybe Abigail just wants a little for herself. Like a child vying for the grownups' approval, she pipes up, "I did it too! I did it too!"

Her long silence during Tituba's confession may, however, have a more sinister explanation. She knows now what "pretense" Salem is, and she sees a chance to pay back the hypocrisy of "all these Christian women and their covenanted men" with a monstrous trick. Tituba just got away with a vicious attack on her uncle; might not Abigail be able to do the same with her enemies? All she has to do is "confess" and anything she says will be believed. The temptation for revenge is too irresistible.

But let's not get carried away in making Abigail the villain of this piece. Remember the atmosphere in the room, remember how frightened they all are. Tituba has just been released from a crushing burden of guilt. Abigail, too, has sinned, and she knows it. Whatever she does later, at this moment she may long fervently for "the light of God" and "the sweet love of Jesus."

However you interpret Abigail's confession, it does bring Betty back to life. Hale is jubilant: "Glory to God! It is broken, they are free!" As Putnam rushes out to summon the marshal, Hale shouts above the din, "Let the marshal bring irons!"

The madness has begun.

ACT II

ACT II, SCENE 1

Act I began in a state of tense anxiety, and built steadily to an orgy of excitement. Act II, by contrast, opens with an air of tranquil domesticity. It is dusk, and upstairs a woman is singing a lullaby to her children. The kitchen fire spreads its soft light about the darkening room, and above the embers hangs an iron pot full of bubbling stew.

Into this peaceful scene comes John Proctor, home after working all day in his fields. The children are going to sleep, and Elizabeth Proctor now comes down to serve up her husband's supper. This could be any time in history, any place in the world. The Proctors could be any mother and father relaxing at last together at the end of a long day. They make small talk about the boys, about the farm. Nothing could be more "normal."

Only the slightest hints of trouble disturb this placid picture: Elizabeth's stew lacks flavor; John kisses her but she doesn't respond very warmly; she forgets to give him cider to go with his meal; there are no flowers in the house. These little things may seem unimportant, but we notice them. We already know this marriage hasn't been perfect—John Proctor did have an affair with Abigail Williams. Maybe he had a reason. Twice in Act I Abby said Elizabeth is a "cold, sniveling woman." Could there be some truth in this description? Now the woman herself is before us. Let's see what she's like.

Her first words are, "What keeps you so late?" Maybe she's only worried that something happened to him. He wanted to finish seeding the farm, he replies, and this seems to satisfy her for the moment.

But if she has more on her mind, his lateness will come up again.

For the next few minutes John tries everything he can think of to get her to warm up toward him, but the only time she smiles is when he says the stew is well seasoned (and we know it wasn't). Finally, he has to know what's wrong: "I think you're sad again. Are you?" Sure enough, she's still bothered by his being late. The rest of the scene will bring out everything that makes this marriage so shaky.

NOTE: The Abigail-Proctor-Elizabeth triangle is perhaps the most important subplot of the play, because it's these three people that we follow most closely through the next three acts. But the main story is the development of witch madness in Salem, and we cannot be allowed to forget it for long.

Here we see Arthur Miller's ingenuity with "exposition," often the hardest thing a playwright has to do. He must tell us what's happened offstage or in the past, things we need to know in order to understand what happens onstage. Eight days have passed since the end of Act I, and somehow we need to know all that has happened in the meantime. But Miller can't be too obvious or clumsy. The worst kind of exposition is to have one character say to another, "As you know, the following things happened in the last eight days. . . ." He might be able to make it a little less awkward by changing the line to, "Did you hear what happened in the last eight days?" but the audience will still recognize what he's doing and say, "Oh, here comes the exposition."

What Miller does instead is get us thinking about something else entirely, in this case, what's wrong between John and Elizabeth Proctor. And part of what's wrong is that John's been to Salem once already, and there he saw Abigail. Elizabeth must be wondering if it really is over between her husband and this girl; maybe he went to see her again and that's why he was late. What she's really worried about is that John still loves Abigail, but Elizabeth doesn't yet have a good reason to accuse him of this directly. Besides, John hasn't been to town in more than a week. But Mary Warren has, and the stories she brings back are hard to believe. Elizabeth is carefully working up to something as she tells John about the court, the judges, the fourteen people already in jail, the talk of hanging. Who's the cause of this madness? "Abigail brings the other girls into the court, and where she walks the crowd will part like the sea for Israel."

You see what's happened? While we're waiting for Elizabeth to spring the name of Abigail, Arthur Miller has slipped the exposition in by the side door, as it were.

Elizabeth puts her husband to a test: he must go to town and tell them this witchcraft business is a fraud. Of course he hesitates, afraid no one will believe him. But Elizabeth doesn't see it that way: "John, if it were not Abigail that you must go to hurt, would you falter now? I think not."

Now it's out. But Proctor's fed up with her suspicion and her coldness, and tells her bluntly, "Let you look to your own improvement before you go to judge your husband any more. . . . Learn charity, woman."

Suppose you've done something you're ashamed of, something that badly hurt a person you love very much. You can say that you're sorry and you'll never do it again, and you'll try everything you can think of to make up for it. Of course you know things may never be the same again, but when months go by and the person you hurt still hasn't forgiven you, it's understandable that you'd begin to resent it. This is how John Proctor feels.

It's easy to sympathize with him in this scene. He did wrong, but he confessed it, and Abigail was put out. And he has "gone tiptoe in this house all seven month since she is gone." But "still an everlasting funeral marches round [Elizabeth's] heart." Nobody's perfect, and enough's enough.

Let's not forget, though, that the last time we saw Proctor, he was with Abigail, and he admitted looking up at her window and that he still may think about her softly from time to time. And he did *not* say, "I don't love you anymore." This is the real issue to Elizabeth—not the wrong he did before or the right he's trying to do now, but how he still feels in his heart about Abigail. We know she's got good reason to worry.

ACT II, SCENE 2

Before this issue can be brought completely out in the open, Mary Warren comes home from court. This scene does several important things: 1) it interrupts John and Elizabeth's argument just when it was coming to a head, keeping us in suspense until they can resume; 2) it brings us new information about the trials and what happens in court; and 3) the poppet Mary gives to Elizabeth sets up the "proof" that will lead to Elizabeth's arrest at the end of the act.

NOTE: Of these three things, Mary's descriptions of the trials is most crucial, for now we see how the witchcraft works. A person is cried out for a witch and is arrested and brought into court. We've already seen

Hale go to work on Tituba, so we know what court examinations are like—denials are useless. But Mary's story adds a new wrinkle:

> . . . she sit there, denying and denying, and I feel a misty coldness climbin' up my back, and the skin on my skull begin to creep, and I feel a clamp around my neck and I cannot breathe air; and then I hear a voice, a screamin' voice, and it were my voice. . . .

The witch has "sent her spirit out" to torment the girls who have accused her. This will turn out to be the most damning evidence against an accused witch. It sounds crazy to us today (as it did to Proctor and some others at the time), but the judges had good reason for putting so much stock in "spectral evidence," as they called it. Listen to Deputy Governor Danforth, in Act III:

> In an ordinary crime, how does one defend the accused? One calls up witnesses to prove his innocence. But witchcraft is *ipso facto*, on its face and by its nature, an invisible crime, is it not? Therefore, who may possibly be witness to it? The witch and the victim. None other. Now we cannot hope the witch will accuse herself; granted? Therefore, we must rely upon her victims—and they do testify, the children certainly do testify.

The only way to refute such logic is to deny the existence of witchcraft. But then you're left with the question, What *is* tormenting these children? And for that, no one has an answer.

Mary also tells the Proctors that Goody Osburn will hang, but that Sarah Good will not, *because she confessed*. This is extremely important—the last act of the play revolves around this legal procedure. A bit later in this act, Proctor will say to Reverend Hale, "There are them that will swear to anything before they'll hang; have you never thought of that?" It's a question that will come to haunt him later, when the noose is threatening his own neck. It is already beginning to haunt Reverend Hale, as we will find out. Hale hasn't come in yet, but let's remember this question when he does.

John Proctor's having enough trouble in his own house without worrying about the nonsense going on in the town. And now this serving girl refuses to stay at home as he commanded her to do. It's the last straw, and he goes for his whip. But Mary's an official of the court now, she says, and she'll not stand whipping any more. Besides, she saved Elizabeth's life today by saying she never saw any sign of witchcraft about the house. The whip comes down unused, and Mary Warren goes to bed.

ACT II, SCENE 3

This last revelation casts a whole new light on John's relationship with Abigail. The scene that follows is the most intense confrontation between two people in the play. They no longer have time for fooling around; if John and Elizabeth must settle with each other, it's now or never.

The danger is clear to both of them: Abigail means to cry out Elizabeth for a witch. What are they going to do? Proctor says he will go to the court and tell them what Abigail said to him. But Elizabeth is a woman, and she understands Abigail better than John does: Abigail thinks she still has a chance with John, if only Elizabeth can be removed. So John must go to Abigail and call her a whore, kill any hope she might have of ever getting him for herself. He agrees, but it makes him mad. He says, "it speaks deceit, and I am honest!"

What does he mean by "deceit"? That he still loves Abigail, and that calling her a whore will be a lie? Or that he thinks this is a cheap trick? He doesn't explain. He goes back to his old complaint about Elizabeth: "I see now your spirit twists around the single error of my life, and I will never tear it free!"

But Elizabeth knows what to think:

> You'll tear it free—when you come to know that I will be your only wife, or no wife at all! She has an arrow in you yet, John Proctor, and you know it well!

NOTE: The Puritans' views on sex were not so "puritanical" as we usually imagine. Sexual intercourse between married persons was not only encouraged, it was required by law. If a husband proved impotent, his wife could have the marriage annulled. If the wife refused sex to her husband, this was considered "neglect of duty" and could be used as grounds for divorce. God had commanded his people to be fruitful and multiply, and the Puritans took this commandment seriously.

Today we call sexual intercourse "making love," or "sleeping with." To the Puritans, a man and woman who had intercourse were "made one flesh." If you were married, it was your duty to be made one flesh with your spouse. But if you were made one flesh with someone other than your spouse, this was adultery. And adultery, like witchcraft, was a capital offense. Elizabeth Proctor must love her husband very much to keep his secret. Later we will see how much Proctor loves Elizabeth—he is willing to confess to adultery in order to save her.

ACT II, SCENE 4

Reverend Hale comes in on a curious errand: "to put some questions as to the Christian character of this house, if you'll permit me." How changed he is from when we saw him last! Then he was bold and confident; now he seems tentative, almost shy. He is obviously troubled by the developments of the last few days. He, too, like Mary Warren, is an official of the court. But she is merely a witness. He is a judge. His signature is on Goody Osburn's death warrant. But he's a stranger to these people, and things are beginning to move too fast for him.

Keep your eye on Hale. In a way he's our stand-in or proxy—we, too, are strangers in this town. His reactions will be much the same as ours would be if we were in his shoes.

Hale loves the truth more than anything in the world. This love made him a scholar in the first place. It has also sharpened his sense of what's *not* true. And he's begun to feel uneasy about what's happening in Salem. It's just a feeling, and a vague one at that, but before he signs another death warrant he wants to know whom he's sending to the gallows.

We already know Proctor doesn't think much of Salem's minister, Samuel Parris. But church attendance is compulsory by law, and if Proctor's youngest son dies unbaptized, he will go straight to hell. Hale has a right to be worried about this "softness" in John Proctor's record.

Worse yet, Proctor cannot recite the Ten Commandments. Remember Mary Warren telling us that Sarah Good couldn't do it either. And Sarah Good's been "proved" a witch, first by sending her spirit out in open court, later by confession. Proctor does a little better—he gets all but one, the seventh: Thou shalt not commit adultery. This is a serious failing, because the Puritans believed that all of God's laws are summarized in the Ten Commandments.

You've probably had the experience of blanking out on a test. You know the answer, it's on the tip of your tongue, but no matter how hard you try to think of it, it just won't come. Hale seems to realize that this may be the case here; he decides to let it pass, even though he has misgivings.

Proctor then tells him what Abigail said, that "the children's sickness had naught to do with witchcraft." Hale is shocked, and wants to know why Proctor has kept this information back. The answer Hale gets alarms him more than anything he's heard tonight. Proctor doubts the existence of witches, and Elizabeth agrees with him. Witchcraft is Hale's specialty, remember, and he knows that the first thing a witch will say is not, "I am no witch," but "There's no such thing as a witch."

Notice two things in this passage. The first I've already mentioned, the fact that some "will swear to anything before they'll hang," and Hale knows Proctor's right in saying this. The second thing occurs when Proctor assures Hale that Elizabeth is incapable of lying. Abigail, in Act I, repeatedly called Elizabeth a liar. But Abigail, as we've seen, is a liar herself. On the other hand, Proctor, in Act III, will repeat his claim that Elizabeth cannot tell a lie, and it will ruin them both. Arthur Miller is here preparing us for that catastrophe.

ACT II, SCENE 5

Things begin to happen very quickly. Giles Corey and Francis Nurse come in; their wives have been arrested. In one very short scene we find out that: 1) No one is safe, if these two godly women can be accused; and 2) The accusers are seeking revenge—on Rebecca Nurse for murdering Goody Putnam's babies, and on Martha Corey for murdering Walcott's pigs. These two facts can add up to only one thing: Elizabeth Proctor is next.

ACT II, SCENE 6

Sure enough, Ezekiel Cheever, clerk of the Court, appears at the door, followed by Marshal Herrick. The trap has been sprung on Elizabeth. The poppet Mary Warren made out of boredom, to fill the long hours of sitting in court, and then gave to Elizabeth to make up for being so long away from home, is now the "hard proof" that Elizabeth is a witch. It's ludicrous that a doll would cause a woman to hang. What signifies a poppet?, everyone wants to know.

NOTE: Dolls, teddy bears, and the like play a large part in the lives of most young children. You probably had one yourself, and remember playing games and having elaborate conversations with it. Puritan children were no different from other children in having dolls to play with. Poppets were not in themselves anything to worry about, or else how could Mary Warren make one in full view of the judges and the court?

But in one respect a poppet was suspicious. A child could have a poppet, but a grownup keeping one was unnatural. Witches were widely believed to make images of their victims in order to torment them from a distance. The witch would stick a needle or thorn into the body of the image, and that part of the victim's body would be wracked with searing pain. Stick the needle in the image's heart, and the victim was supposed to die.

Why would Abigail dare to do something as outrageous as this? Several answers are possible: 1) she's gone crazy and doesn't know what she's doing anymore; 2) she's drunk with the power she's acquired and is seeing how far she can go in leading grownups by the nose; 3) Elizabeth is right, "she'd dare not call out such a farmer's wife but there be monstrous profit in it. She thinks to take my place."

Hale's position at this moment is critical. He's a figure of authority, not only as a judge, but as a specialist in witchcraft. If Abigail's trick gets past him, she's likely to get away with it, and Elizabeth Proctor will hang for being a witch.

We know, as the Proctors know, what Abigail is up to. Whatever her motivation, she stuck that needle in her belly herself. But how do we know? First, by circumstantial evidence: we saw Mary Warren give the poppet to Elizabeth just moments before Hale arrived. Elizabeth hasn't left the room since then, so if she had stuck the needle in the poppet, we'd have seen her. More important, we know Abigail Williams—what kind of person she is, what she wants—and we believe she is capable of trying to frame Elizabeth.

Hale is in the dark on both these points. When he entered the Proctors' house for the first time in his life, that poppet was sitting on the mantelpiece and could have been there for years for all he knows. As far as he's concerned, Abigail Williams is what he sees every day in court: a young girl writhing in agony on the floor, suffering so hideously that it breaks his heart and fills him with rage against her tormentors.

For all his learning and keen intelligence, the Reverend John Hale also has a tender heart, and it is this, if anything, that makes him falter now. It's hard for him to believe that women of such spotless reputation as Rebecca Nurse and Martha Corey could be witches. It means, as he says, that "nothing's left to stop the whole green world from burning." But he can't discount the possibility. He's seen too many "wonders" in court.

And the alternative is appalling. To believe Proctor is to "charge a cold and cruel murder on Abigail." This is why, when Mary Warren tells him the real story of the poppet, he asks her, "May it be, perhaps, that someone conjures you even now to say this?" It's a reasonable question; he's seen it happen in court. Mary answers, "Why, no, sir, I am entirely myself, I think," and adds that Abby saw her make the poppet and stick the needle in. This is troubling information, but Hale is too uncertain of himself among these strangers; he dare not leap to the conclusion that is so obvious to us.

And so Hale, the intellectual with the soft heart, misses his chance to save the lives of innocent people. But maybe some of them are not so innocent. Before he leaves, Hale tells an enraged John Proctor:

> . . . I cannot think God be provoked so grandly by such a petty cause. . . . Man, we must look to cause proportionate. Were there murder done, perhaps, and never brought to light? Abomination? Some secret blasphemy that stinks to Heaven? Think on cause, man, and let you help me to discover it. For there's your way, believe it, there is your only way, when such confusion strikes upon the world . . . think on your village and what may have drawn from heaven such thundering wrath upon you all.

It's the only thing he can think of to explain what's going on: someone is hiding a sin so disgusting it has called down God's punishment on the whole community. These words strike straight into John Proctor's heart.

ACT II, SCENE 7

Mary Warren is now Proctor's only hope to save Elizabeth. He will do anything; he will sacrifice Mary and himself, but "that goodness will not die for me!"

There is something almost demonic in the violence of Proctor's rage. Earlier he had demanded of Hale:

> Is the accuser always holy now? Were they born this morning as clean as God's fingers? I'll tell you what's walking Salem—vengeance is walking Salem. . . . I'll not give my wife to vengeance!

Now he goes to Salem to accuse, to "charge a cold and cruel murder on Abigail." Are his motivations "holy"? Is there no vengeance in his heart? He seems almost to look forward to his own destruction, as long as he can bring Abigail down with him: ". . . her saintliness is done with. We will slide together into our pit."

But maybe he sees this as a chance finally to get the punishment he feels he deserves for his sin of adultery; a punishment Elizabeth denied him by keeping his secret. If this is the case, it could be relief he's expressing when he says,

> Peace. It is a providence [blessing], and no great chance; we are only what we always were, but naked now.

ACT III

ACT III, SCENE 1

Act III is a courtroom drama. We've been hearing a lot about this court; now we will see it in action. Arthur Miller has prepared us for the coming battle between the witch-hunters and their victims. We now know all the principal characters, where they stand and what they want. All the subplots have been laid out: 1) Parris and the "faction" bent on ousting him; 2) Thomas Putnam's greed for more land; 3) Ann Putnam's poisonous envy of Rebecca Nurse; 4) Hale's struggle with his conscience; 5) Abigail's deceitfulness and her designs on John Proctor; 6) The trouble in the Proctors' marriage; and 7) Mary Warren's dilemma of being caught in the crossfire. The outcome of all these plots will be decided in this act. As Mr. Hale once said, "You will witness some frightful wonders in this room, so please keep your wits about you." But everything's so complicated, how can we do that?

NOTE: A courtroom drama is a lot like a football game. First of all, there are regulations: things nobody can do, things certain players can do but others can't, penalties for breaking these rules. There are yard lines, out-of-bounds lines, and goal lines. When the ball is snapped, everybody takes off in a different direction. If you've never seen a football game before, it must look like utter chaos. But at the end of each play, the ball is usually in a different place, and you can tell which way and how far it's been moved.

It's hard to watch a game and not take sides. You don't watch a game just to see who wins, but to see if your team will win. And you want your team to win; you cheer when it does well, and your heart sinks when the other team does better.

The longer you watch, the more you learn about the rules, almost without knowing it. Of course you want to know how well your team is playing, but you also become interested in *how* they're playing (What plays are they running? Is the other team playing fair?).

A courtroom drama works in much the same way. In the first place, there are two sides—prosecution and defense—and only one side can win. Usually we've already taken a side before the trial itself starts. Because we care which side wins, we follow each argument closely, look for loopholes, and try to anticipate how the case will unfold.

In Act III we have on one side the victims of the witch-hunt, represented by John Proctor. On the other we have the witch-hunters themselves. The difference between this courtroom drama and most others is that the court itself is one of the contestants. The court, in effect, *is* the witch-hunt. Without it there would be no arrests, no jailings, no trials, no convictions, no hangings.

If John Proctor loses his case, he and all the people who support him will be destroyed. Reverend Parris repeatedly accuses Proctor and his followers of trying to overthrow the court. We may not like Parris very much, but here he's telling the truth. For Proctor to save himself and his friends, he has to convince the court that everything it has done so far is wrong. And if the court is wrong, then a lot of people have suffered—and some have been put to death—for nothing. If Proctor wins, all belief in the court will be destroyed, and the judges themselves could be charged with murder.

The odds against Proctor are overwhelming, but there is reason for hope. First of all, Proctor has the truth on his side. Abigail actually told him there was no witchcraft involved. We also know that Proctor is willing to risk everything—his good name, even his life—to bring this truth out. Second, Deputy Governor Danforth, for all his sternness, is an intelligent and just man. He will give Proctor a fair hearing, even though it may mean the total overthrow of the court.

Some say that the outcome of this act depends on the answer to the question, "What kind of man is John Proctor?" Before Danforth can decide on the charges, he must know the man who brings them. If you interpret it this way, then the action of this act consists of an examination of John Proctor's character. Each event or argument is then "evidence" that supports one of two opposing positions: 1) John Proctor is a good man, and is therefore telling the truth; or 2) John Proctor is an agent of the Father of Lies, so naturally he's lying.

During the examinations, Danforth takes Proctor seriously at every point. He *has* to, Proctor's charges go right to the heart of what is most important here: justice. Danforth wavers only when Abigail and the girls go into their "torments." He is clearly frightened by these girls, but he manages to keep his head until Mary Warren defects to Abigail's side. Then Danforth turns to Proctor and demands, "What are you? You are combined with anti-Christ."

This last point about Mary Warren hints at another way of looking at Act III. In 1692, a farmer like John Proctor would most likely have a cart for carrying things around. Each wheel on the cart would be held in place by a linchpin, which was stuck through a hole in the axle on the outside of the wheel. Under normal circumstances a linchpin doesn't have much work to do. It just has to keep the wheel, as it turns, from "walking" off the end of the axle. But if the wheel goes over too many bumps, the linchpin can loosen and fall out. It can also be sheared off, if too much pressure is put on it.

According to this interpretation, Mary Warren is the linchpin of Act III. She cannot withstand the pressure that is put on her—from Proctor on one side, Abigail on the other, and hard questioning by the judges in the middle. It's difficult to imagine anyone not breaking under the strain.

NOTE: The setting of this act is curious. If this is a courtroom drama, why are we not in the courtroom? But remember that the court itself is on trial. When the court is in full session, with the jury and the whole town looking on, the judges at the bench have absolute power. Giles Corey tries to present his evidence in open court, and gets himself thrown out for disrupting procedure. Perhaps Arthur Miller wants to give the victims a better chance at being heard. He sets this act in the vestry rooms of the meetinghouse, where the judges will be less protected by the trappings of authority.

The first three French scenes of Act III set the stage for the battle that will follow. In Scene 1 we hear Martha Corey's trial in progress offstage.

ACT III, SCENE 2

Scene 2, which begins when Giles Corey is forced out of the courtroom onto the stage, does two things: 1) it lets us know where we are: "This is the highest court of the supreme government of this province"; and 2) it introduces two new characters, Judge Hathorne and Deputy Governor Danforth. Danforth quickly establishes that he's the boss. Everyone is arguing—he settles the argument. He will consider Giles' evidence, but only if Giles follows procedure: "Let him submit his evidence in proper affidavit [in writing]."

This scene also brings out an aspect of the witch-hunt that we've seen before. The most innocent actions can have disastrous consequences: "I only said she were readin' books, sir, and they come and take her out of my house," Giles says, weeping. Giles seems confused. He told Proctor that Martha was arrested for putting a curse on Walcott's pigs. And Danforth obviously knows nothing about Martha Corey and her books.

But really Giles is upset because he "broke charity with the woman." He feels he has betrayed her, and he wants to make up for it. In a way this parallels Proctor's situation with his wife. By committing adultery with Abigail, John certainly "broke charity" with Elizabeth. Both Proctor and Giles Corey are motivated, to some extent, by guilt. This will be extremely important later.

ACT III, SCENE 3

Francis Nurse, the focus of Scene 3, has done nothing to feel guilty about. He is given the job of being the first to tell Danforth that the girls are frauds. Judge Hathorne is just like Reverend Parris—to him "every defense is an attack upon the court," and he wants both Giles and Francis arrested for contempt. But Danforth is a bigger man than that. Francis Nurse has a high reputation, and wouldn't make such a charge lightly. He also has courage: "Excellency, I never thought to say it to such a weighty judge, but you are deceived."

ACT III, SCENE 4

Proctor brings in Mary Warren, the star witness for the defense. A great deal of maneuvering takes place before Danforth agrees to listen to Mary's story. First

John Proctor must be tested. He brought Mary here, and both Francis Nurse and Giles Corey look to Proctor to speak for them. Why is Proctor doing this? Danforth wants to know. Just to save his wife? Apparently not, because Proctor won't drop the charge even after he finds out Elizabeth is pregnant and is therefore safe for a year or more. And his charge is shocking: the children are lying. If this charge is true, it will mean that seventy-two people have been condemned to hang on the basis of lies. This will undermine the authority of the court, and Danforth will be lucky to escape Salem with his life. So he must be absolutely certain Proctor is to be taken seriously.

Once he is convinced of Proctor's sincerity, Danforth proceeds to investigate the charge without hesitating. Considering what he has at stake, this is courageous.

Proctor has built his case carefully. He has prepared three depositions, or written statements, which he hopes will win the court over. This shows good strategy: if the first deposition has little effect, bring in the second; if that's still not enough, bring in the third.

The first statement backfires; everyone who signed it will now be arrested. The second fares worse: Giles Corey accuses Thomas Putnam of "reaching out for land." Putnam is brought in, and of course denies it. Giles, seeing what happened to the people who signed the first petition, refuses to reveal the source of his information. And then he makes matters worse by trying to catch Danforth in a legal technicality. This angers the deputy governor, who declares the court in full session. Now all that's left between the victims and disaster is the third deposition, Mary Warren's.

But before Mary's ordeal begins, let's check up on Reverend Hale. Remember he's our proxy, he stands in for us in this play. You'll recall how much he changed in the week between Act I and Act II. Another week has passed; has Hale changed still further? In one way he is still the same. When anyone gets excited, Hale's the first one to try to calm things down. But now there's an added note of desperation in his pleas for peace, as if he's afraid he himself might be losing control. Notice what he's saying. In Act II he defended the court against the outrage of the farmers. Now he's defending the farmers against the sternness of the judges. He supports Giles Corey's outburst; he protests that every defense is not an attack upon the court; he tries to excuse Giles' silence by saying "there is a prodigious fear of this court in the country"; and he thinks Proctor's "weighty claim" should be argued by a lawyer.

In all of these attempts he is brushed aside. Perhaps this explains his desperation: he sees this situation drifting toward disaster, and he is losing—or has already lost—his power to stop it.

Now for Mary Warren. Proctor has no doubt coached her in what to say. We know she is afraid of him, we have seen him threaten her. But he knows that threats alone won't stiffen Mary against the gruelling trial she will have to face. He has encouraged her as well. He tells her a Bible story in which an angel watches over a little boy who also faces a dangerous task. He reminds her of all the good people who are behind her all the way. He has even set up their plea so that Francis Nurse and Giles Corey will go up against the court first; these men will surely convince the judges that Mary should be given a sympathetic hearing. And behind all this moral support is the rock wall of the truth. If all else fails, Proctor must have told her, she has truth on her side. Because God damns all liars, Abigail and the other girls are going straight to hell. Mary may even be able to save her friends from eternal torment, by breaking up this conspiracy of lies.

But in the end, as Mary well knows, everything will depend on whether or not the judges believe her story. The weakness of her story is obvious to everyone. She says the girls are lying. How does she know? Because she used to be one of the group. If we believe her now, it means she was lying before when she cried out witches with the rest. But if she was a liar then, how can we believe her now?

ACT III, SCENE 5

To answer this question, Danforth brings in Abigail, Mercy Lewis, Susanna Walcott, and Betty Parris. This is horribly unfair—four against one—but in a way there's no alternative. Somebody's lying here, and the only way to find out who is to face Mary with those she's accusing.

Even if Proctor's plan had worked and the first two depositions hadn't backfired, the whole weight of his charge would still rest on the slender shoulders of Mary Warren. If Abigail will not confess to lying—and from what we know of her this is unlikely—we'll have a case of Mary Warren's word against the girls'. And as Danforth says, "I have until this moment not the slightest reason to suspect that the children may be deceiving me."

In all fairness to Danforth, here he is bending over backward to give Proctor's charge the benefit of the doubt. Much about Proctor is suspicious: his wife's in jail; he doesn't come to church but plows on Sunday; Mary's obviously been threatened by him, even though she denies it. And Mary is a confessed liar— that is, if she's telling the truth now. Despite all these doubts, Danforth turns to the girls and urges them to tell the truth.

Notice how he speaks to them. All Mary Warren got from him was sharp questions, full of accusation. To the girls, Danforth's tone is considerate, almost respectful. He tells them Mary's charge, then lets them know just how suspicious of her he is:

> . . . it may well be that Mary Warren has been conquered by Satan, who sends her here to distract our sacred purpose. If so, her neck will break for it.

He follows this up with the weak assurance that "a quick confession will go easier with you."

Danforth's unconscious prejudice is not lost on Abigail. He has just told her whom he wants to believe, so she tells him flatly that Mary is lying.

But Proctor won't let it be settled so easily. "What may Mary Warren gain but hard questioning and worse?" he asks, knowing this question is in Danforth's mind as well. Then Proctor goes on the attack: Abigail is no child, she laughs at prayer, she leads other girls out to dance naked in the woods. This is all news to Danforth, and he looks at Abigail with fresh eyes.

But then Judge Hathorne, who so far has been kept in the background by Danforth's superiority, comes up with an ingenious idea. If Mary was only pretending before, let her pretend now, let her give them all a demonstration of how she deceived the court. Of course she can't do it. Who could, under such circumstances?

NOTE: Remember the discussion of the girls' fits in Act I. Modern research shows that one of the best ways to cure mass hysteria is to isolate its victims from

one another. This was actually tried in Salem in 1692:
one of the youngest of the afflicted girls was sent to
Beverly, where she stayed with Reverend Hale's wife
and two daughters. Within a few weeks she had
calmed down almost completely. Perhaps this is Mary
Warren's problem here: she's been "cured by her
week away from the other girls. She's lost the *sense* of
it now, as she says.

Hathorne and Parris think they have won. Mary
has failed the test, so she must be lying now. But
Danforth isn't sure. Too much doubt has been cast on
Abigail, and Mary's pathetic explanations somehow
ring true to him. So he turns to Abigail again and bids
her search her heart and speak the truth.

But Hathorne's trick has brought Abigail enough
time to collect her wits. Once again, as she did with
her uncle in Act I, she dodges the question and attacks
Danforth for asking it, even going so far as to threaten
him openly:

> Let *you* beware, Mr. Danforth. Think you to be so
> mighty that the power of Hell may not turn *your*
> wits? Beware of it!

The irony is that this is precisely what's happening.
Abigail Williams, at this very moment, is turning Danforth's wits toward her destructive purpose.

But she breaks her threat off in midsentence.
Maybe she's afraid of going too far, maybe she just
gets a better idea. It is fun twisting Danforth around
her little finger, but Danforth isn't Abigail's real enemy here, Mary Warren is, and Mary Warren must be
destroyed. What better way then to "cry her out"?

We've heard a lot about the awful torments these
poor girls endure in court day after day. Now we get
to see them in action. The important thing here is not

what these girls suffer, but *who* is being made to suffer. To the judges, these are children. Adults are strong enough to fend for themselves; but the suffering of children is an outrage.

Danforth cannot conceive that a child could be evil enough or even smart enough to plot murder. Abigail knows this, and she plays on it. When it begins to look like Proctor might be opening Danforth's eyes, Abigail moves quickly. And the girls, like robots, follow suit.

They haven't lost the "sense of it," as Mary Warren quickly sees. By now the girls are old hands at being tormented, and can turn it on as easily as a water faucet. They follow Abigail's lead, each one building on the other's fantasy until they've worked themselves into a proper "torment"—cold skin, chattering teeth, shivering from the same "icy wind."

The judges' reaction is automatic. They've seen this happen before, they know what it means. Danforth immediately wheels on Mary Warren:

> Mary Warren, do you witch her? I say to you, do you send your spirit out?

It's a brilliant move on Abigail's part, but it almost blows up in her face. Proctor, seeing Mary's nerve give out, is driven to the wall. In a total rage he leaps at Abigail and jerks her up by the hair. "How do you call heaven! Whore! Whore!"

Now it's out, and Proctor's done for. Whether Abigail is exposed or not, Proctor's just destroyed himself. There's no way he can win. But maybe by unmasking Abigail he can save his wife and his friends.

Danforth's shining image of Abigail has been tarnished, but this new charge of Proctor's is too shocking. It must be proved. So Danforth sends for Elizabeth Proctor.

ACT III, SCENE 6

Elizabeth knows nothing of what's happened in the room, but she senses almost immediately that this is a test. What's going on is not entirely clear to her, except that John's in trouble and his fate depends on her answers to Danforth's questions. From where we sit, it's amazing that Elizabeth doesn't see the trap. But remember what she's been through in the last week: arrested in the middle of the night and hauled off in chains to jail; tried as a witch, with the girls in full cry throughout the trial; convicted and sentenced to hang; allowed no contact with the outside world, especially her husband. If she's exhausted and confused, it's not surprising. And if she's reluctant to even open her mouth, it's no wonder at all—every word she's said so far in her own defense just set the girls to howling all the louder.

But even if she has her wits about her, her mistake is easy to understand. She can see where Danforth's questions are headed, but she doesn't know who talked. John may have confessed, but isn't it far more likely that Abigail, out of sheer spite, accused John first?

Whatever Elizabeth's reasoning, she fails the test. She tells Danforth that her husband is no lecher. As Hale says, it's a natural lie to tell; she thought only to save her husband's name. But Danforth will have none of it. Proctor claimed that his wife couldn't tell a lie; very well, Elizabeth has just cleared Abigail. And Proctor's charge against Abigail was nothing but a last-ditch effort to overthrow the court.

If you think for just a moment, this makes no sense at all. If Proctor is a liar, then saying that Elizabeth cannot lie could itself be a lie. Elizabeth also denied being a witch; Danforth obviously thinks this is a lie, or he wouldn't have found her guilty and sentenced her to hang. Why should he believe her now, when she denies her husband is an adulterer?

One answer can be found near the end of the previous scene. In a stage direction Arthur Miller describes Danforth as "Himself engaged and entered by Abigail." This means that she has him somehow hypnotized, and that whatever Elizabeth answers, he'll see it as letting Abigail off the hook. If Elizabeth says, "Yes, Abigail's a whore," it could merely be a plot by the witch and her husband to discredit the court's chief witness against her.

There's another possibility, that Danforth's "wits have been turned," just as Abigail threatened. If this is the case, then he simply no longer knows what he's doing.

Don't forget that the court has based every one of its decisions *solely* on the "testimony" of Abigail and the girls. If Abigail has been lying, the court is destroyed. Danforth may be taking "any port in the storm" to keep his world from collapsing. Proctor cannot prove his charge, therefore the charge is false. Abigail is vindicated, the court is saved, and the witch is dragged back to her cell.

ACT III, SCENE 7

If Danforth were to be allowed a little time to think, he might be able to see how flawed his logic is in this situation. But Abigail knows better than to give him this chance. Hale has openly thrown himself on Proctor's side: "I believe him! This girl has always struck me false!" She moves fast, turning on a "torment." This time it's not a vague cold wind coming out of nowhere; it's a yellow bird with sharp claws, and its name is Mary Warren.

This is too much for poor Mary. Her protector has been destroyed, and her strength is gone. At last the truth itself deserts her, because no one will believe it. With her defenses down all around her, Mary "catches" the affliction herself. When Proctor tries to help her, "she rushes out of his reach, screaming in horror":

> Don't touch me—don't touch me! . . . You're the Devil's man!

Proctor is finished, and with him goes the last hope for his wife and friends. Realizing this, Proctor bursts out with one of the most despairing speeches in modern drama:

> I say—I say—God is dead! . . . A fire, a fire is burning! I hear the boot of Lucifer, I see his filthy face! And it is my face, and yours, Danforth! For them that quail to bring men out of ignorance, as I have quailed, and as you quail now when you know in all your black hearts that this be fraud— God damns our kind especially, and we will burn, we will burn together.

This speech comes at the end of a crescendo of excitement, like a volcano erupting. It's hard to imagine a more perfect opportunity for the playwright to put his "message" across. To some, that is exactly what this speech is: the author's thematic statement. The key phrase here is, "For them that quail to bring men out of ignorance. . . ." Proctor is blaming himself as well as the others for this catastrophe. He should have stopped this madness when he had the chance. Arthur Miller is telling his audience: Don't be like John Proctor. Come out against superstition (in this case, McCarthyism) wherever you find it, and do it now, before it's too late. If you're looking for the "message" of the play, here it is.

Others see more here than just the author using Proctor as a mouthpiece. Of course, *what* Proctor says is important. But isn't there something familiar about his emotional state when he makes this speech? Haven't we heard someone *sound* like this before?

Look at Tituba's "confession" near the end of Act I:

> . . . Mr. Parris must be kill! Mr. Parris no goodly man, Mr. Parris mean man and no gentle man, and [the Devil] bid me rise out of my bed and cut your throat!

Even closer to hand, just moments before there was a similar outburst from Mary Warren:

> Don't touch me—don't touch me! . . . You're the Devil's man! . . . I'll not hang with you! I love God, I love God. . . . "I'll murder you," he says, "if my wife hangs! We must go and overthrow the court," he says! . . . He wake me every night, his eyes were like coals and his fingers claw my neck, and I sign, I sign . . .

There is even a kind of echo of the rhythm of Mary's speech in Proctor's "A fire, a fire is burning!" and "we will burn, we will burn together." We have the same explosion of pent-up fury, and the same calling down of destruction. Tituba rages at Parris; Mary attacks Proctor. Proctor, caught in the same trap, turns his wrath on everyone. He is saying, in effect, "the world is insane. Blow up the world."

NOTE: This is almost pure "nihilism." The word *nihil* in Latin means "nothing." Proctor is calling for annihilation, not just of himself, but of Danforth, the court, and the entire community. This interpretation says that there is no simple or easy way to stop the spread of this kind of madness once it starts. The only way to save Salem now is to demolish it.

However you look at Proctor's speech, it definitely marks the conclusion of the main story. The suspense is over. The forces of madness have triumphed, our hero is destroyed, and the witch-hunt will continue. It may burn itself out, or go on forever—there's nothing to stop it anymore.

ACT IV

ACT IV, SCENE 1

At the end of every play the loose ends have to be handled. This is called the "denouement." Usually it comes in the last few minutes of the play, following the catastrophe, that moment when the hero's fortunes hit bottom.

In a way, all of Act IV of *The Crucible* is denouement. The catastrophe occurred at the end of Act III when Proctor was betrayed by Mary Warren. Things can't get any worse. But there are still loose ends, and Arthur Miller uses Act IV to tie them up. He does this by once again focusing on the relationship between John and Elizabeth Proctor. They have not seen each other in the three months that have elapsed since Act III. Considering what their last meeting was like, their reunion is likely to be intense.

But first it must be set up. In this first scene we see two deranged women, Tituba and Sarah Good, being cleared out of their cell by a drunk Marshal Herrick. Apparently something important is about to take place, because it's the middle of the night.

NOTE: In one short stroke Arthur Miller sets the mood and hints at what's happened in the last three months. A cow bellows outside the window, and both women jump up and answer, thinking it's the

Devil finally come to take them home. The ordeal those poor souls have been through has unhinged their minds. They have taken refuge from the insanity of the real world in a blissful fantasy of singing and dancing where it's always warm and the "Devil, him be pleasureman in Barbados."

But Herrick knows it's not Satan, "just a poor old cow with a hatful of milk." It's a strange image, a cow in the middle of the town, complaining through the night because she hasn't been milked. We'll soon find out what it means.

ACT IV, SCENE 2

After Tituba and Sarah have been removed, Danforth and Hathorne come in, followed by their stolid assistant, Cheever. In this brief scene we hear some troubling news. Reverend Hale has returned after denouncing the court. Hathorne reports that Reverend Parris seems to be losing his grip. And Cheever explains about the cow:

> There be so many cows wanderin' the highroads, now their masters are in the jails, and much disagreement who they will belong to now.

In other words, Salem is falling apart. Almost everyone who speaks from now on will do variations on this theme, building an image of the community in total disintegration.

ACT IV, SCENE 3

Reverend Parris enters and explains that Reverend Hale is praying with the prisoners, to get them to confess. Danforth takes this as good news. But Parris isn't finished. Abigail and Mercy Lewis have disappeared. They stole all Parris' money and took passage on a ship three days ago. By now they are well out of reach. And Parris thinks he knows why. A rumor has hit Salem that the neighboring town of Andover "have thrown out the court . . . and will have no part of witchcraft." The girls got out before the storm hit here.

Parris' life has been threatened already, and he's afraid that Salem will riot if they hang Proctor and Rebecca Nurse today. But Danforth will not postpone the executions.

ACT IV, SCENE 4

Reverend Hale comes in to add his plea to Parris'. The prisoners will not confess; he must have more time. Danforth explains why he won't postpone. Things are uncertain enough; if the court falters the least bit now, there is real danger of losing control of the situation. But a confession will secure the court's position. He sends for Elizabeth Proctor. Maybe she can persuade her husband to confess.

Once again, notice how Hale has changed. In Act III he was near the edge, but up until the very end he hung onto the belief that he was doing the right thing by helping the court. But when Proctor was condemned, it was the last straw.

Now Hale has returned, but for what purpose?

> Why, it is all simple. I come to do the Devil's work. I come to counsel Christians they should belie themselves. There is blood on my head! Can you not see the blood on my head!!

This recalls Giles Corey's anguished cry at the beginning of Act III: "I have broke charity with the woman." The difference is that Hale has "broke charity" with a lot more than one person. And now he must break charity with God, by counselling them to lie in order to save their lives.

ACT IV, SCENE 5

We see the depth of Hale's disillusionment and disgust with himself when he pleads with Elizabeth to get Proctor to confess:

> Beware, Goody Proctor—cleave to no faith when faith brings blood. . . . Life, woman, life is God's most precious gift; no principle, however glorious, may justify the taking of it.

Here is another speech that looks like a good candidate for "author's thematic statement." And it's spoken by the man who's most like us.

But Hale by now is a lost soul. A minister of God, he is counselling people to lie. How can we have faith anymore in anything he says? Elizabeth senses this, and tells him, "I think that be the Devil's argument."

Besides, it's a useless subject to dispute. Elizabeth has more pressing business on her mind than theological arguments. She must see her husband one last time. She has something to tell him.

ACT IV, SCENE 6

This scene is not long, but a lot happens in it. In terms of the plot, it's pretty simple: John explains to Elizabeth why he's going to confess. She urges him to do what he has to do, and tells him that no matter what he decides, he's a good man. That's it.

We know from Danforth that Proctor's confession is important to the court and the town. But John doesn't seem to care much what his confession means to anyone but his wife. And Elizabeth doesn't seem to care whether or not he confesses at all.

What's really going on in this scene has little to do with events in the outside world. In Act II Arthur Miller made us part of the emotional life of John and

Elizabeth's marriage. We not only care what these
people do, we want to know what they feel. John
Proctor will either confess or he won't. If he does, it
won't be in this scene. For the moment, the important
thing is to find out what's in their hearts.

The first half of the scene is all small talk, as it was in
their first scene together, the opening of Act II. Now,
as then, we get "exposition": Elizabeth is healthy,
John's been tortured, the boys are taken care of, no
one who matters has yet confessed, and Giles Corey
was pressed to death. They run out of news, and a
silence falls. Then John begins to explain himself.

His main reason for confessing is, as he puts it, "I
cannot mount the gibbet like a saint. . . . Nothing's
spoiled by giving them this lie that were not rotten
long before." He feels unworthy to die with the others, for they are truly innocent people. But he wants
Elizabeth to forgive him for this lie he's about to tell.
He wants her to "see some honesty in it." In other
words, he wants her to judge him. This is a far cry
from Act II when he warned her angrily to learn some
charity herself before she judged him.

Of course, a lot has happened since then. But none
of it could have meant more to him than the one lie
that Elizabeth told in her life, the lie she thought
would save her husband's name. When Danforth
asked her if her husband was a lecher, the two words
"No, sir" contained all her love for John. And how
could he hear those two words without it breaking his
heart?

Elizabeth has also changed. She cannot judge him
any more:

> John, it come to naught that I should forgive you,
> if you'll not forgive yourself. It is not my soul,
> John, it is yours.

Of course, beneath all this talk of confessing or hanging is another sin than lying. And that's what Elizabeth really wants to talk about:

> I have read my heart this three month, John. I
> have sins of my own to count. It needs a cold wife
> to prompt lechery.

She is telling him that whatever he did in the past is forgiven. He has more than proved his love for her. Now she wants him to know her love.

This "confession" of love is more important to her than John's decision to confess or hang. Without the love she now shows him, either choice he makes is a lie. Her love confirms his goodness:

> Whatever you will do, it is a good man does it.

John doesn't seem to get it. He's carried his guilt around for so long that he's used to it. In Act II he accused her of twisting her spirit around the single error of his life. But it's his spirit, not hers, that has become twisted by guilt. He has come to think of himself as totally corrupt because of this one mistake. It will take some convincing for him to accept Elizabeth's new vision of John Proctor, the man who is good no matter what he does. And they have no time.

One thing has happened: Abigail is forgotten. Her name is never mentioned; she has no power over either of them anymore. Whatever lies in the future, they are now free from the shadow of suspicion and guilt that chilled their marriage. John and Elizabeth Proctor are reconciled at last.

ACT IV, SCENE 7

Hathorne comes in and Proctor says he'll confess. It's a shaky decision, and he still feels he needs Elizabeth to back him up. But she has given him his freedom; she won't take it back now, though his choice breaks her heart.

Hathorne, of course, is electrified by the news. He runs out shouting to the world that Proctor will confess. But John continues to agonize. Has he made the right decision?

> I think it is honest, I think so; I am no saint. Let Rebecca go like a saint; for me it is fraud!

He is still fishing for Elizabeth's support. Why is he so unsure of himself? His thinking is sound, all his reasons are the right ones. A travesty of a court convicted him of a crime that doesn't exist, and even if it did, he didn't commit it. The only thing that's real is that rope out there. Hale said it: life is God's most precious gift. What possible reason could John have for throwing it away? Pride? How dare such a sinner as he is have so much pride?

Remember Elizabeth's answer to Hale. This is the Devil's argument, and Proctor knows she would never fall for it herself. But he still thinks of her as "that goodness." He believes he knows himself better.

> It is evil. Good, then—it is evil, and I do it!

Here is an echo of the same nihilism we heard at the end of Act II and Act III. Elizabeth's love hasn't saved him yet.

ACT IV, SCENE 8

Danforth bustles in with Hathorne, Hale, and Parris. Cheever follows with paper and pen to take down the confession. Proctor is horrified at their efficiency and glee; he hates giving these "dogs," as he calls them, what they want. But though his jaws lock on him for a moment, he gets out the basics: the Devil came to him and bid him do his work on earth. Proctor won't get any further than this in his confession.

NOTE: All of Act IV has been leading up to this moment. But let's stop and think. Isn't there a problem with these "confessions" in the first place? Remember in Act II, when Mary Warren first described the witch trials, she said that Goody Osburn would hang, but that Sarah Good was saved because she confessed?

In most legal systems, confession is considered conclusive proof of guilt, meaning no other evidence is necessary to convict the accused. Conviction leads to sentencing, and in this case the law clearly states what the punishment for witchcraft is to be: "Thou shalt not suffer a witch to live." Sarah Good convicted herself when she confessed. How is it that she is "suffered to live"?

The flaw in the logic is obvious, as we noted in the discussion of Act II. "There are them that will swear to anything before they'll hang," as Proctor said then, and as he is thinking of doing now. If the court is really trying to get at the truth, it just doesn't make sense to offer such an irresistible inducement to life.

But remember how difficult it is to prove the "invisible crime" of witchcraft. There are only two witnesses, the witch and the victim. If the judges can get the witch to confess, it will release the victim from suffering, and spare the judges a difficult decision. In addition, a confession is, *ipso facto*—to use Danforth's terminology—a renunciation of witchcraft. With a confession, the judges not only spared a victim, they rescued a soul from hell.

This reasoning doesn't completely answer the objection, but it does give some idea of how the judges see the situation. Hathorne may be narrow-minded and bitter, but he's not blood-thirsty. And Danforth is more concerned than anyone with doing the right thing—not only legally, but as a man who has considerable power over the souls of others.

ACT IV, SCENE 9

For this reason, he has Rebecca Nurse brought in to witness Proctor's confession. Proctor has great standing among the condemned, and if Rebecca can be persuaded to join him in confessing, maybe the others will follow, and no one will have to hang this morning.

It'll never work. As Elizabeth says, Rebecca has one foot in heaven already, nothing can hurt her now. Proctor is filled with shame under Rebecca's astonished gaze, though he tries to keep going in the evil he's decided to do. He hits a snag when he's asked to name others he's seen with the Devil.

NOTE: Up until now, every confession the judges received implicated others. Naming names proved the witch was now on God's side and wanted to do everything possible to defeat the archenemy Satan. Inside information on the Devil's "troop strength" was obviously the most valuable service a repentant witch could provide.

We saw it happen at the end of Act I, when the girls, prompted by Tituba, reeled off names in a frenzy. If every witch did the same in her confession, it's easy to see why this madness spread as fast as it did.

Proctor can't do it. "I speak my own sins; I cannot judge another," he says. Hale and Parris, though for different reasons, talk Danforth into accepting this much as sufficient.

Then Proctor has to sign it. He resists, but Danforth has bent enough for this man. John Proctor signs his name.

What finally gets to him is that this lie, with his signature at the bottom, will be posted on the church door for the whole world to see. He knows it doesn't make sense, but that's where the line is for him—he just can't cross it:

> Because it is my name! Because I cannot have another in my life! Because I lie and sign myself to lies! Because I am not worth the dust on the feet of them that hang! How may I live without my name? I have given you my soul; leave me my name!

This is a stirring speech. If you've ever been in a situation where you've reached your limit and can't stand any more, you'll recognize the feeling John Proctor is expressing.

NOTE: But what does he mean, "I have given you my soul; leave me my name"? Surely his soul is more important than two words on a piece of paper.

It used to be that a man's "name" meant his reputation. The name of Rebecca Nurse, for example, was synonymous with goodness, kindness, common sense, and peacemaking. The name of John Proctor, before the disaster of his trial, meant strength, honesty, and fair dealing. Is this what Proctor is trying to protect?

Maybe, and maybe more. These people want to use his confession to continue the witch-hunt. It's bad enough they've destroyed him, but he can't let them use his name to destroy others.

And there's also the possibility that Proctor means something more fundamental. There is one Bible verse that John probably knew well.

> And out of the ground the lord God formed every beast of the field, and every fowl of the air; and brought them unto Adam to see what he would call them: and whatsoever Adam called every living creature, that was the name thereof.
>
> (Genesis 2:19)

Before man, nothing had a name. A man's name is a symbol of his unique position in God's creation. Take away John Proctor's name, and he is *nothing*.

So he rips up his confession. Between Elizabeth's great love and the judges' intolerable demands, John Proctor has found himself. His guilt, his doubt, his nihilistic rage are gone. What remains is

> . . . some shred of goodness in John Proctor. Not enough to weave a banner with, but white enough to keep it from such dogs.

He kisses Elizabeth, and goes out with Rebecca to be hanged. Hale pleads with Elizabeth frantically, but she knows she has won:

> He have his goodness now. God forbid I take it from him!

A STEP BEYOND

Tests and Answers

TESTS

Test 1

I. Parris is worried because   _____
   - I. Betty is sick
   - II. he caught the girls dancing in the woods
   - III. Abigail was fired by the Proctors
   - A. I and II only
   - B. II and III only
   - C. I, II, and III

2. Proctor doesn't like Parris because the minister   _____
   - A. is a coward
   - B. is too quiet
   - C. is materialistic

3. Tituba confesses that   _____
   - A. she saw Sarah Good with the Devil
   - B. she tried to kill Reverend Hale
   - C. she committed adultery

4. John Proctor considers himself a sinner because   _____
   - A. he was cold to Elizabeth
   - B. he committed adultery with Abigail
   - C. he hit Mary Warren

5. In the woods, Abigail wanted   _____
   - A. a charm to kill Elizabeth
   - B. a frog
   - C. to dance naked

6. The judges at the trial were   _____
   A. Corey and Hale
   B. Danforth and Parris
   C. Danforth and Hathorne

7. "I'll not be ordered to bed no more, Mr.   _____
   Proctor! I am eighteen and a woman,
   however single!" is said by
   A. Elizabeth Proctor
   B. Mary Warren
   C. Abigail Williams

8. Abigail and the girls get Mary Warren to   _____
   rejoin them by
   A. threatening to kill her
   B. appealing to their old friendship
   C. pretending she is sending her spirit out
      to harm them

9. Elizabeth is not hanged because   _____
   A. she is pregnant
   B. she bribed the judges
   C. she is innocent

10. Abigail   _____
    A. becomes a respected housewife
    B. is hanged
    C. runs away

11. Describe the Puritan theocracy.

12. What were the beliefs concerning witchcraft in Salem in
    1692?

13. How did Reverend Parris contribute to the witch mad-
    ness?

14. How is witchcraft presented in *The Crucible*?

Test 2

1. Which of the following statements are *not*   _____
true?
> I. Tituba is blamed for the death of
> Mrs. Putnam's babies
> II. Rebecca is considered a bad person
> by many people
> III. No one is ever actually hanged as a
> result of the trials

A. I, II, and III
B. II and III only
C. I and III only

2. The commandment John Proctor has broken   _____
is
A. Honor thy father and mother
B. Thou shalt not bear false witness
C. Thou shalt not commit adultery

3. John takes back his confession because   _____
A. he wants to save his reputation
B. he wants to protect Elizabeth
C. he is hoping to escape

4. One theme of *The Crucible* is   _____
A. true love always wins out
B. all's well that ends well
C. pretense is destructive

5. At the end of the play, Proctor gains a   _____
victory by
A. confessing
B. tearing up his confession
C. refusing to accuse Parris of witchcraft

6. The protagonist of this play is   _____
A. Rebecca Nurse
B. Reverend Parris
C. John Proctor

7. Proctor tries to justify his confession by   _____
   A. saying he is innocent
   B. saying he is already a sinner
   C. blaming Abigail for his troubles

8. In the last scene, Hale wants to   _____
   A. convince John to confess and save his
      own life
   B. go to Andover to find more witches
   C. run away with Abigail

9. At the end of the play, the words that best   _____
   characterize John Proctor's conscience are
   A. confused and desperate
   B. calm and certain
   C. troubled and regretful

10. Who among the following is not listed with   _____
    his or her ultimate fate?
        I. Rebecca is hanged
       II. Giles Corey is hanged
      III. Parris is voted from office
    A. I and II only   B. II only
    C. I and III only

11. Why is Reverend Hale important?

12. Why doesn't John Proctor confess?

13. Compare Reverend Samuel Parris to Reverend Hale.

14. What is the significance of the title?

ANSWERS

Test 1

1. C   2. C   3. A   4. B   5. A   6. C
7. B   8. C   9. A   10. C

   11.   The Puritans left England in the 1620s, fleeing from
religious intolerance, and hoping to establish God's "visible

Kingdome" in the New World. There they formed a "theocracy"—literally, a government by God—which was supposed to enforce God's laws. These laws were written down in the Bible, and were summarized in the Ten Commandments. Every man, woman, and child in the colony was supposed to know these commandments by heart, and act accordingly.

Church attendance was compulsory, even for "strangers"—visitors, traders, in fact everyone but the Indians, who had not been officially confirmed by the church. Newborn babies had to be baptized as soon as possible; if they died unbaptized, they went straight to hell.

Public punishment was one way the Puritan theocracy maintained its authority. Whippings, hangings, and being made to stand in the stocks for hours in the town square were common.

The leaders believed their power came from God, and it was their duty not only to maintain order and promote well-being in the colony, but to keep a sharp eye on their citizens' spiritual lives as well.

12. The belief in the Devil—God's archenemy, sometimes called Satan—was widespread among the Puritans of colonial Massachusetts. The Devil had once, according to legend, been the brightest among God's angels (another name for the Devil was Lucifer, which means "Lord of Light"). But he was jealous of God's son Jesus, so Satan rebelled and started a war in heaven. He lost, and was cast into hell, where he and his followers set up their own kingdom. From there the Devil continued his war on God. And one of his favorite targets to attack was God's favorite creature, man.

Satan and the other fallen angels, sometimes called demons, stalked the earth in various disguises, trying to corrupt as many men and women as they could. Like a stranger offering candy to a child, the Devil held out won-derful temptations to those who would follow him. But they were all lies: as soon as the misguided witch died, he or she was whisked straight to hell to be tormented forever.

But before that, a witch had a duty to get more followers for his or her master, and to punish anyone who resisted. One way a witch could torture an innocent soul was to "send her spirit out" to pinch, stab, burn, or just terrify her victim. Another was to make a likeness in the form of a doll or "poppet," and hold it over a fire or stick it with pins, thereby tormenting the victim from a distance.

13. Reverend Parris had a lot to do with the contention that was already boiling in Salem before the witchcraft started. He thought of himself as the innocent victim of a conspiracy to oust him from his pulpit. There had been con-siderable wrangling over his election in the first place, and bitterness still hung in the air between the rival factions. The group that had not wanted Parris had gone to another church, and the ones who stayed insisted on keeping his salary low. Parris used his pulpit to harangue his enemies and bully his supporters into giving him such things as money for firewood and a deed of ownership to his house. John Proctor complained that Parris ranted and raved until he got golden candlesticks on the altar in the church, and that he had no qualms about damning to hell anyone who disagreed with him.

When the witchcraft first broke out, Parris was terrified that his enemies would ruin him with it, because his daugh-ter Betty was the first to be afflicted. He soon found, how-ever, that by siding with the witch-hunters, he could even the score on some old grievances.

14. Arthur Miller doesn't really say whether he believes in witchcraft or not. But he does take great pains to give a rational explanation for everything the Salemites say is witchcraft. Tituba's "confession" of witchcraft is her only way out of an impossible situation: everyone already believes she is a witch, so she has no choice, if she doesn't want to hang, but to "confess."

Even Abigail, who so ruthlessly manipulates the madness for her own ends, starts off in much the same way. She's in trouble, and sees confessing as a way to get out of being whipped or worse. The other girls' "torments" can be explained as a case of mass hysteria—as soon as one "catches it" it quickly spreads to the others. We also see how easily they can slip in and out of these torments once they get the hang of it.

Test 2

1. A   **2.** C   **3.** A   **4.** C   **5.** B   **6.** C

7. B   **8.** A   **9.** B   **10.** B

11. In a way, the whole witch madness was Hale's fault. When he was first invited to Salem by Reverend Parris, it was only to determine if there was witchcraft afoot or not. But by taking himself and the girls—whom he had never met before—too seriously, he led them into acting "witched."

Afterward when the situation began to turn into a nightmare, Hale missed several chances to stop the spread of witch madness by pondering too long and trusting too much in the righteousness of the court. By the time he realized that the court itself was mad, it was too late, and his only course of action was to denounce it, a weak gesture at best.

In the end he returned and tried to make up for the damage he'd caused, by counselling prisoners to "confess" and save their lives. But this had little effect, and the witchcraft came to an end only when it had burned itself out.

12. There was a legal paradox in the Salem witch trials: a witch who confessed was saved, while someone who denied being a witch was hanged. Many people took the obvious choice and lied to save their necks. Why didn't John Proctor do the same?

At first, he kept silent out of spite: "It is hard to give a lie to dogs." He does think about confessing, but not for the usual reason. For him it would be a worse lie to die like a saint with Rebecca Nurse, because, as he says, "I am not worth the dust on the feet of them that hang." He even gets so far as signing his name to a dictated confession, but he rips it up when he realizes his jailers want to use his name to carry on the witch-hunt.

This act of sacrifice for his friends, though it doesn't stop the witch-hunt, doesn't do it any good. Proctor sees a shred of goodness in this, and goes willingly to the gallows.

13. The only thing that Parris and Hale have in common is their profession—both are ministers of God, with degrees from Harvard Divinity School. But Parris took up the ministry in middle life, having first been a merchant in Barbados (where he acquired Tituba). Hale, on the other hand, has been a minister all his adult life. In addition, Hale is a scholar, having studied deeply in demonology, and has a widespread reputation for "high learning."

The biggest difference between the two is their temperaments. Parris is a narrowminded, suspicious, and self-centered man. His main concern in any situation is how it affects him. This is especially clear in the opening scene, when he is less worried about his stricken daughter Betty than about how his enemies will use the witchcraft to drive him from his pulpit. Later, in Act III, he calls everyone's defense an attack upon the court, and tries to use the court's authority to get back at his enemies. In the end, he gets his comeuppance when Abigail flees with all his money, and even Judge Danforth calls him a brainless man.

In contrast, Reverend Hale is mostly concerned with the truth, and with providing for the greatest good for all of God's creatures. Although his belief in witchcraft is as strong as the others', it comes from years of study, not superstition. He comes to Proctor's house in Act II because he feels uneasy about signing death warrants for people he does not know. In the last act he comes to the prison to persuade the condemned prisoners to confess, even if it means lying. This is a tremendous act of self-sacrifice—everything he once believed in must be thrust aside to save these people's lives.

14.   Arthur Miller first thought of calling his play *Those Familiar Spirits*, which refers to the "spirit" a witch supposedly "sends out" to torment her victims. By changing the title to *The Crucible*, the author broadened the meaning of the play.

A crucible is an earthenware pot or bowl used for melting down metal. In the Middle Ages alchemists (who were often associated with witches) used the crucible in their search for a way to turn baser metals into gold. Today, a crucible is the name given to the well at the bottom of a blast furnace where the molten steel collects. Whatever is in a crucible therefore is subjected to tremendous heat and its solid structure is completely broken down. This is a perfect metaphor for what happened in Salem in 1692.

Another meaning of the word crucible is "a severe trial or test." This would certainly apply to John Proctor, whose "goodness" is put to the ultimate test. He can do evil by "confessing" and live. But in the end he chooses to die rather than "give a lie to dogs."

Term Paper Ideas

Social Drama

1.   Compare the 1692 Salem witch hunt with the Communist "witch hunt" of the 1950s in America. Were the investigations and trials conducted differently? Was a particular type of person singled out for persecution?

— **2.** What social conditions made such a thing as the Salem witchcraft possible? Do any of these conditions exist today? If so, is there a chance that this might happen again?

3. *The Crucible* had little effect in stopping the "Red-baiting" it was written against. Why do you think it failed? Was there anything Arthur Miller could have done differently in writing the play to make more people listen to him?

Personal Tragedy

1. Discuss the love triangle of Elizabeth-John-Abigail. What effect does this tense relationship have on each character? What effect would it have on the community if it were made public?

2. Compare Elizabeth Proctor with Abigail Williams. How well do they understand each other? What does John see in each of them? What makes John reject Abigail and confess to Elizabeth?

3. Discuss Proctor's "nihilism," or desire for destruction. Where does it come from? How does he escape from it and find his "goodness" in the end?

4. In Act IV, Elizabeth tells John Proctor that "whatever you will do, it is a good man does it." What does she mean? What is the "shred of goodness" that he finds in himself when he tears up his confession?

Hysteria

1. The outbreak of witch madness in Salem was tiny compared to the mania that ravaged Europe for two hundred years before and after 1692. Compare the American version to its European "model." Did they start differently?

Is there any reason the Salem witchcraft was over so quickly, while in Europe it raged for years, killing thousands as compared to Salem's twenty?

2. What are the psychological conditions that are necessary to produce mass hysteria? Are we immune today?

Superstition
1. What is the religious background of the Salem witchcraft? Were these people fanatics who were half-crazy anyway? Or were they noble visionaries who somehow went astray?

Greed and Vengeance
1. How much of what happened in Salem can be blamed on cold-blooded manipulation of events for the purpose of profit or revenge? Is it possible today that a few greedy and/or vengeful people could instigate another witch-hunt?

Authority
1. Discuss the concept of authority under the Puritan theocracy. Who were the powerful? And how did they get their power?

2. Part of what went wrong in Salem came from a dispute over who had the authority to decide whether or not witchcraft was being practiced in a particular instance. How did this dispute arise? How was it resolved? How is authority presented in *The Crucible*?

3. Is Proctor's downfall ultimately caused by what the judges see as his rebellion against authority?

Theocracy
1. Compare the theocracy of the Puritans with the looser form of government in Virginia at the same time. Which was better? Which was more successful?

2. What are the problems inherent in a theocracy? Whose interpretations of God's law are right and whose wrong? Is it possible to govern people's spiritual lives as well as their physical lives?

Justice

1. Nearly all of Arthur Miller's plays have one character who is connected with the law—a policeman, a judge, a lawyer. Compare these characters. Taking them in order, is it possible to see a pattern or development in Arthur Miller's thinking about justice?

2. Hale says in Act IV: "Life is God's most precious gift; no principle, however glorious, may justify the taking of it." Do you agree?

3. Is there *no* justice in what happened in Salem, even in the long run? Did any good come of it?

Historical Drama

1. Arthur Miller has taken quite a few liberties with history in writing *The Crucible*. Why did he change what he did? How could he have done it differently?

2. Despite the way they dress and the language they speak, John and Elizabeth Proctor strike many people as thoroughly modern characters. Do you agree? What about them or their situation is modern, and what makes them purely a man and woman of their own time and place?

General

1. There are a lot of similarities between *The Crucible* and another play by Arthur Miller, *After the Fall*. What makes John Proctor and Quentin so much alike? How are they different?

2. Is there real evil stalking Salem in 1692? Where is it? How does it work?

3. Put yourself in Salem in 1692. Would you have joined the witch-hunt? What would you have done if someone cried you out as a witch?

4. Arthur Miller has done a lot of experimentation with nonrealistic styles of playwriting. Compare *The Crucible* with either *Death of a Salesman* or *After the Fall* in terms of style and structure. What are the advantages and disadvantages of each? Is there anything that can be said in one way and not the other?

Further Reading

CRITICAL WORKS

Bentley, Eric. *The Dramatic Event*. Boston, 1954.

Corrigan, Robert W., ed. *Arthur Miller, A Collection of Critical Essays*. Englewood Cliffs, N.J.: Prentice-Hall, 1969.

Huftel, Sheila. *Arthur Miller: The Burning Glass*. New York: Citadel Press, 1965.

Martine, James J., ed. *Critical Essays on Arthur Miller*. Boston, G. K. Hall, 1979.

Weales, Gerald, ed. *The Crucible: Text and Criticism*. New York: Penguin, 1977.

Welland, Dennis. *Arthur Miller the Playwright*. New York: Methuen, 1979.

AUTHOR'S OTHER WORKS

Plays

The plays are given in chronological order, by date of publication. The year of first production is in parentheses.

All My Sons (1947). New York: Reynal and Hitchcock, 1947.

Death of a Salesman   (1949). New York: Viking, 1949.

A View from the Bridge   (1956, revised two-act version of original one-act play). New York: Dramatists Play Service, 1957.

Arthur Miller's Collected Plays.   New York: Viking, 1957. Contains *All My Sons, Death of a Salesman, The Crucible, A View from the Bridge,* and *A Memory of Two Mondays.*

After the Fall   (1964). New York: Viking, 1964.

Incident at Vichy   (1964). New York: Viking, 1964.

The Price   (1968). New York: Viking, 1968.

The Portable Arthur Miller   (edited with an introduction by Harold Clurman). New York: Viking, 1972. Contains *Death of a Salesman, The Crucible, Incident at Vichy,* and other writings—stories, reportage, and a poem.

The Creation of the World and Other Business   (1972). New York: Viking, 1973.

The American Clock   (1981). New York: Dramatists Play Service, 1982.

Fiction

Focus.   New York: Reynal and Hitchcock, 1944. A novel.

I Don't Need You Any More.   New York: Viking, 1967. A short-story collection.

Scripts for Film and Television

The Misfits.   New York: Viking, 1961. A screenplay-novel.

Playing for Time.   New York: Bantam, 1981. Teleplay.

Nonfiction

The Theater Essays of Arthur Miller   (edited with an introduction by Robert A. Martin). New York: Viking, 1978. See especially: "Journey to *The Crucible,*" pp. 27–30; "Brewed in *The Crucible,*" pp. 171–174; "Arthur Miller: an Interview," pp. 290–92; and "It Could Happen Here—and Did," pp. 294–300.

The Critics

I speak of "sin." It is an unfashionable word nowadays and Miller rarely uses it. He is . . . sufficiently imbued with the skepticism of modern thought to shy away from the presumptions implicit in it. But that Miller is willy-nilly a moralist—one who believes he knows what sin and evil are—is inescapable.

> —Harold Clurman, Introduction to
> *The Portable Arthur Miller*, 1972

Despite its realistic form, *The Crucible* is less dramatic realism than a modern morality play, in which the characters are intended to be dramatized symbols of good and evil. My only reason for doubt . . . is that [George Bernard] Shaw was even more devastating about intolerance in *Saint Joan* by giving its representatives a sound logical case and making them good and conscientious men, and then showing the horrifying results of what they did.

> —Richard Watts, Jr., Introduction to
> *The Crucible*, 1959

In my play, Danforth seems about to conceive of the truth, and surely there is a disposition in him at least to listen to arguments that go counter to the line of the prosecution. There is no such swerving in the record, and I think now, almost four years after writing it, that I was wrong in mitigating the evil of this man and the judges he represents. Instead, I would perfect his evil to its utmost and make an open issue, a thematic consideration of it, in the play.

> —Arthur Miller, Introduction to *Arthur Miller's Collected Plays*, 1957

With John Proctor . . . Miller goes for something deeper than the one-dimensional "good guy." Proctor is enough a product of his society to think of himself as a sinner for having slept with Abigail Williams; so he carries a burden of guilt before he is charged with having consorted with the devil. When he is finally faced with the choice of death or confession, his guilt as an adulterer becomes confused with his innocence as a

witch; one sin against society comes to look like another. The stage is set for another victim-hero, for a John Proctor who is willing to be what men say he is, but at the last minute he chooses to be his own man.
—Gerald Weales, *Arthur Miller's Shifting Image of Man*, 1967

The "evil" in the play focuses on Abigail as fountainhead. . . . Her wickedness . . . amounts to a shrewd use of the hypocrisy, greed and spite that thrive in her neighbors under the pretext of seeing justice done. Her power arises from her ability to convert her psychic energies and the willful pursuit of her own objectives into a genuine visionary hysteria. At bottom Abby knows that her prophetic fit is self-induced, that the witchcraft she denounces is non-existent; but once the fit is on her, she can produce a convincing performance and induce the same kind of hysteria in the children. Her real diabolism is her misuse of the sacrosanct office of witness to gain her own ends.
—Thomas E. Porter, *The Long Shadow of the Law*, 1969